CELTIC FISTS

CELTIC FISTS

Michael Prestage

Foreword by
Barry McGuigan

The Breedon Books
Publishing Company
Derby

First published in Great Britain by
The Breedon Books Publishing Company Limited
Breedon House, 44 Friar Gate, Derby, DE1 1DA.
1997

Published with the kind permission of S4C, TnaG, HTV and Grampian TV

ISBN 1 85983 110 9

Printed and bound by Butler & Tanner Ltd., Selwood Printing Works, Caxton Road,
Frome, Somerset.

Colour separations by RPS Ltd, Leicester.

Jackets printing by Lawrence-Allen Colour Printers, Weston-super-Mare, Avon.

Acknowledgements

Book based on the series
Celtic Fists
produced by Concordia Cyf for
S4C
Teilifis Na Gaeilge
HTV Wales
Grampian TV

Photographs for this book were supplied by
AllSport, PA News Photo Library, Popperfoto,
Sporting Pictures, Universal Pictorial Press &
Agency.

Contents

Foreword
by Barry McGuigan

CELTIC boxers are different from the Anglo Saxons. We are more tenacious, more determined and tougher. The Celt also has more of a firebrand nature that lends itself well to boxing.

Throughout boxing history the Celts have been especially drawn to the ring because of their lowly social and economic status and because it offered a chance to compete on an equal footing. Here was true equality of opportunity.

I think the records through the decades show it. From the Irishman John L. Sullivan being proclaimed the first World heavyweight champion to Steve Collins, the Celtic Warrior, fighters from Ireland, Scotland and Wales have dominated.

They bring the volatile nature of the Celt into the ring with them. That is why we have provided the best fighters from these shores, although I'm obviously going to be a bit biased.

The Celtic crowds willing their fighters on are also something else. I have experienced that intoxicating atmosphere at Belfast and Dublin.

Indeed, when I returned to Dublin after winning the World featherweight title in London from Eusebio Pedroza, I attracted a crowd comparable to that which greeted the Pope.

I have witnessed some incredible scenes since. The last time was in Cardiff, when the local fighter Steve Robinson fought, and the partisan support he received was amazing.

It has to be said there is also that element of self destruction that applies to the Celts perhaps more so than others.

Although for all boxers the rags to riches to rags story is more often than not the way things turn out. The lives of 90 per cent of boxers end up a catalogue of disasters. People once national heroes finish their lives destitute.

And sadly, although the training and preparation for fights is better and more rigorous health checks are in place, there are still the unscrupulous in boxing who look to exploit fighters. There are those who still take advantage of boxers.

That is why, as president of the Professional Boxers Association, I and my colleagues are trying to ensure the best help and advice is available for young fighters from people like myself who have been there, seen it and bought the T-shirt.

It is not easy. Boxers tend to be shortsighted and they are irrevocably independent. The idea of a union is often anathema to them. Boxing is not a team sport, but it is important to have the association there working for them and that is being realised by more and more fighters.

Celtic boxers are not just fighting themselves out of poverty and oppression. They can galvanise their respective nations and communities, bringing pride and passion and a shared sense of belonging.

Satellite television has brought a wider audience. When I fought Pedroza, 200 million viewers worldwide followed the fight with 20 million in the UK and Ireland alone. The money at stake has also soared.

But the nature of the sport is largely the same — the ultimate gladiatorial combat between two finely-tuned athletes.

As you will see from this book, the fight game has turned up some truly great Celtic fighters, some wonderful characters and, sadly, some tragedies that bring the whole brutal business into focus.

For more than a century, Celtic boxers have taken their

place among the sports elite. Long may it continue. There are undoubtedly more chapters to be written about the Celtic history of boxing.

Introduction

EVERY truly great boxer has been fuelled by deprivation. The history of the ring is the story of young men squaring up to poverty, some paying the ultimate price for a burning desire to escape their surroundings.

At its best the ring dramatises a world of victory for the socially downtrodden. It offers colourful, satisfying rituals that embody the most profound human striving and always presents them in merciless, unsentimental terms.

Boxers respond to violent surroundings by embracing violence. By accepting brutality and returning it with interest. By being as tough and savage as their environment.

There are a few notable exceptions. The fight game has occasionally attracted those whose background was not working-class poverty or from an immigrant influx with a need to fight to survive. In the 18th century, the bare-knuckle champion of England, Daniel Mendoza, was a boxing coach to Lord Byron. The American writer Ernest Hemingway was a great boxing fan and liked to take to the ring.

At the highest level, the Welsh lightweight World champion in the years of World War One, Freddie Welsh, came from a well-off background. His father was an auctioneer and in his early fight days he adopted the name Welsh so his family would not know he was boxing.

In the main, though, those with a moneyed or privileged

background have a spectating role in the fight game. Those who box choose to do so because they have a stark choice — as in the case of the British heavyweight champion Tommy Farr. For him it was boxing or the coal mines.

The Celtic nations on the western shores of the British Isles are one of the world's premier pugilistic breeding grounds. Harsh and brutal working-class life requires a dramatic form to express its reality. Boxing acknowledged, rather than denied, life's cruelty. It even celebrated it. The sport brought order to bloodiness. It made it comprehensible by confining it to two men who fought by rules and who represented larger communities.

Throughout boxing history the Celts have been especially drawn to the ring because it offered a chance to compete against Englishmen on an equal footing.

The list of Celtic champions is a long and honourable one, from the Welsh greats of Jimmy Wilde, Freddie Welsh and Jim Driscoll in the early years of the century, to Steve Collins, the Celtic Warrior, who still reigns as WBO super-middle-weight champion.

English fight fans will no doubt be reeling-off champions from their own history — from the great Ted 'Kid' Lewis in the years of World War One to the strutting genius of Prince Naseem Hamed in the featherweight division today.

There is, though, a depth and quality to the roll call of honour that the Celtic nations have produced that goes beyond nationalistic pleading from the boxing enthusiasts of Ireland, Scotland and Wales. That depth presented some problems in deciding who should be included in this book. The fight game can be a fickle one. Some boxers can catch the public imagination while others with a better pedigree fade from the memory very quickly.

With the Celts dominating British boxing there are many worthy national champions who fail to gain a mention, the Welsh fighters Johnny Basham, Joe Erskine, Dick Richardson and Dai Dower among them. Scottish fight fans with a long memory may tout flyweight Elky Clarke as an omission.

In the main the criteria has been boxers who have been either World champions or had memorable World title fights. But there is also a more subjective category of boxers with a story to tell whose name echoes through the years despite, rather than because of, their fighting reputation. Irish heavyweight Jack Doyle is the best known.

It is hoped the choice of boxers we have included provokes debate rather than irritation and underline the collective strength of the boxing history of Wales, Scotland and Ireland.

Certainly, the boxers themselves are aware of an affinity between the Celtic nations and believe their national heritage gives them an advantage in the fight game.

Barry McGuigan says in the Foreword to this book that he believes Celts are 'more tenacious, more determined and tougher'.

Drew Docherty, the Scottish boxer awaiting his chance for a second World title bout at bantamweight, recalls the instant comradeship between the Celts in the British squad at the 1988 Olympics in Seoul.

"The Celtic countries are more in tune with each other and there is also a definite sense that these are fighting nations," he said. "I feel being a Celt has helped make me the boxer I am."

Gareth Howells, who coached the Welsh amateur boxing team, argues that the Celtic nations have always produced good fighters. "It has been the only way men from these countries could improve themselves. There is no question that in Ireland, Scotland and Wales we have been kept down and exploited."

He remembers in World War Two, a group of black American servicemen stationed in South Wales visiting a tin plate works. On seeing the conditions, one remarked: "I thought we were the slaves." It is, believes Howells, a sad testimony to the position workers found themselves in.

Before irate Englishmen prepare to do battle for their own honour, there have undoubtedly been great English boxers. They will also have come from poor and deprived backgrounds. Such boxing heartlands as the East End of London, Liverpool and Manchester can boast their own fistic heroes.

This book celebrates the boxing greats from the Celtic nations while in no way decrying the efforts of their counterparts in England. It shows that the rise, and ultimate fall, of boxing champions is a depressingly familiar scenario, punctuated with precious few exceptions.

Unfortunately, while it is the boxers who suffer the pain of their bloody business, both in training and in the ring, the profit they deserve rarely comes their way. Too often those who control them, and the purse strings of the money they generate, inevitably seem to outwit the boxers whose reputation and income relies purely on muscle.

Fight history is littered with boxers who find the men who have guided them from their teens, and been father figures, have not had their best interests at heart when the financial arrangements are closely examined.

The great Irish champion Barry McGuigan, whose World featherweight title fights attracted a television audience of millions and generated huge revenue, took his manager Barney Eastwood to court to resolve the issue. The man famed for his reverential 'Mr Eastwood' when discussing his mentor in his younger years, learned in later life to be more questioning.

Few make the effort to go through the courts to win recompense. Of those who do, there is often defeat as the fine print of contracts is studied. McGuigan received £650,000 as money due from previous earnings.

His countryman, Johnny Caldwell, won his bantamweight World title 25 years before McGuigan was crowned king. Even now he speaks bitterly about his dealings with his manager Sammy Docherty. Again the lawyers were involved, but Caldwell lost. He admits he never looked at contracts for fights, but took what he was given.

While it is the case for most that penury awaits them at the end of their fighting days, there are exceptions in the annals of Celtic fighters. Jimmy McLarnin was steered to World title glory in the 1930s by his manager Pop Foster. He succeeded in keeping the money from his big pay days and on Foster's death was bequeathed a further $250,000. McLarnin is still alive and living in California.

There is, of course, an ugly, disturbing side to the culture of the ring. Bare-knuckle fighting attracted some social misfits who revelled in brutality. Boxing is still a potential outlet for bully boys who enjoy inflicting pain, sociopaths who respond only to their own pleasure at others suffering.

Today the unlicensed boxing circuit still thrives, operating outside the jurisdiction of the British Boxing Board of Control, which regulates medical and other standards. At these bouts the welfare of the boxer takes a poor second to providing barbaric entertainment.

The bouts frequently use boxers whose licences have been revoked by the BBBC. Butting, indiscriminate use of the elbow and biting are often featured. The sort of match a

19th-century crowd would have appreciated, but which should have long been consigned to history.

The special order of the ring in properly organised promotions also sometimes breaks down under the tensions it symbolically reconciles, unleashing further violence. In October 1995, a riot broke out among rival supporters fuelled by alcohol at the Holiday Inn, Glasgow, as a boxer, James Murray, lay dying in the ring.

Murray's ambition was to achieve boxing success and to use the cash that came with it to buy his family their council house and his sister a new car for her birthday. The plans for his life were made on the back of his fists. Like others, he paid the highest price for trying fight his way to a better life and win some recognition.

Each death in the ring raises the same old questions about whether there is a place for such gladiatorial contests in modern life. Whether social conditions have improved enough to ensure young men no longer have to take up the sport to fund a better life. The medical profession, for one, certainly sees no need for the fight game in modern society.

The leading boxing writer Ken Jones recalls a fighter in the shower, his mind befuddled from the beating he had taken after a particularly brutal contest, mumbling to his manager: "What round is it?". Such images make it hard to justify boxing as a sport.

Yet boxing can also unite people who would otherwise be at each other's throat. In the 1980s, Barry McGuigan's glorious career crossed the sectarian divide in Northern Ireland at a time when the Troubles were at their height. When the man from Clones was fighting they were united behind one cause.

Boxing can lift a community at its time of greatest need: the crowds who lined the streets of Glasgow in the Depression era of the 1930s to cheer Scotland's first World champion, Benny Lynch, returning in triumph; the post-war gloom in Belfast raised by World champion Rinty Monaghan singing his anthem When *Irish Eyes Are Smiling* after another triumph in the ring. Such sporting moments are long remembered and cherished by those who were there.

Boxers embody a distinctly working-class version of the American dream. Champions fulfil the desire for personal achievement and unlimited individual opportunity, each man testing himself against all challengers, publicly risking injury and humiliation to make it to the top.

Men from poor backgrounds, such as Jim Driscoll, Jimmy Wilde and Tommy Farr, armed only with courage, muscle and skill, became heroes in the industrial valleys of South Wales from which they came. In the south of Glasgow, the legend of Benny Lynch continues 50 years after his death.

Whether they keep their money or not they are still remembered. The largest crowd ever to turn out for a funeral in Wales was not for a politician or military leader, but a boxer. Peerless Jim Driscoll had been born into poverty, but a successful ring career and a generous nature saw him leave as the King of Cardiff.

Few care that it is the lack of other opportunities which pulled these men towards the ring in the first place. Or that most fighters leave the sport as poor and obscure as when they began.

Celtic boxing champions continue to spring from tough neighbourhoods. Prize fighters are now valuable commodities and marketable images. Improved social conditions have not stopped the stream of young men from Ireland, Wales and Scotland, prepared to punch their way to a new life.

For those who make it in the satellite television era, the

rewards are high. The proliferation of titles and weight divisions has given ever more opportunity to hungry fighters. The Celts are primarily a working-class population with men for whom a purse of a few pounds, along with the chance to become a hero among one's peers, is worth the risk of permanent injury and even death.

The legendary boxer and manager Eddie Thomas personified the fighting Celt. A man of many parts, he was almost the stereotypical Welshman: a very good footballer, he sang in the church choir and worked with his father and brothers in the family coal mine. He had a great talent as a boxer, but in his later years thought long and hard about the business he was in for so much of his life. In particular, the dangers involved and the exploitation of the boxers taking part.

Thomas recognised that, despite all their attempts to battle against the environment they were born into, most invariably never escaped. And he acknowledged that there has to be question-marks when the nature of a sport involves attempting to knock an opponent senseless, although in his own boxing days the danger inherent in boxing had never crossed his mind: "It's like a collier going underground. Nobody ever thinks of the danger, although it is obviously there."

During the writing of *Celtic Fists*, Eddie Thomas gave a lengthy interview about boxing and the fighters he had known and trained. It was to be one of his last such interviews, for he died in Merthyr Tydfil, the town where he was born in 1926, on 2 June 1997, after a lengthy battle against cancer.

He won the British, Commonwealth and European championships and trained two boxers, Howard Winstone and Ken Buchanan, to World titles. As will be seen, in the post-war history of Celtic boxers Eddie Thomas figures largely.

Thomas had seen the harsh realities of the boxing world. The politics of the sport denied him his chance of a World title challenge against the legendary Sugar Ray Robinson and left him with a big regret in his career.

Other, more fundamental, issues perturbed him. As a manager and promoter himself, although at heart always more a trainer, he thought more should have been done to protect fighters — often from themselves. From his own days he remembers no fighter ever thanking him for telling him to call it a day.

There were those in the sport for whom boxers were no more than a commodity. A marketable asset. He knew of matchmakers without a care in the world putting fighters in the ring when they were out of their depth.

He remembers Johnny Owen coming to him when he first started, but Thomas's gym was being closed and he was not taking on any more boxers. Brave Owen was to battle courageously in a World title fight with Lupe Pintor in 1980 that cost him his life.

It was Thomas and his wife who arranged to have the body brought back from Los Angeles. No starker reminder of the dangers in the sport is possible. It made Thomas consider his role in boxing. "You wonder whether it was worth it," he said.

Yet with enthusiasm he talks about what makes a champion. And why he believes there is something indefinable in the Celtic spirit that makes them great fighters. That gives them the necessary pedigree.

"People in other professions tell how they live for their work," said Thomas. "It's the same for a boxer only more so. They must have that urge to fight."

He had a simple formula for why he believed the Celts

produce good boxers. "I have always believed in breeding. For a good fighter it is in the blood. When you are breeding a horse or dog, if the breeding is not right it will produce nothing. Take Winstone, he had Welsh, Irish and Jewish blood and they're great fighting bloods. He had to be a champion."

But if the breeding is right for a good fighter, it rarely makes for a good business sense. "Only one in a thousand ever did any good out of boxing. It's frustrating to see fighters battle for everything they have and then lose it all."

He spoke from bitter experience, reckoning to have been conned out of hundreds of thousands of pounds by people he trusted. "It's happened to nearly every fighter I know. I can think of a couple of names who have done all right, but I can't think of any others."

Bringing on boxers and getting the most out of them was the stock in trade of the legendary trainer. And he knew the pitfalls that awaited boxers once success arrived and the cash that came with it.

Thomas knew fighters have to be handled properly, kept away from vices, encouraged to avoid business ventures and the hangers-on who are always there waiting to take advantage. "If you can do that then you have a chance."

Many boxers try to resist the temptations, but few succeed. It is an old boxing adage, but Thomas knew it to be true, that it is hard to become a champion, but even harder to stay there once you are.

He also knew his history. The demise of Benny Lynch, Scotland's first World boxing champion in the 1930s, who was dead of malnutrition and pneumonia by 1946. A brilliant boxer who threw it all away, killed by the bottle. For many others in the fight game, alcohol waits once their fighting days are over.

Thomas stated simply that the greatest danger for the boxer, and particularly the Celtic fighter, is self-destruction. "There is something about boxers and maybe that is also the weakness in the Celt. When you look back and study all these great fighters, self-destruction is the only way they have been beaten. From hangers-on and a weakness for the high life."

Jim Watt, the former lightweight World champion from Glasgow, has his own view on the downhill path Celtic fighters seem destined to take once their careers are over. "They put all their energies into whatever they are doing. When it is boxing that gets their full attention. And when it is drinking, it's the same."

Watt was an exception in that he has kept his money and gone on to a successful business career and worked as a television commentator. He also shares the view that the Celts have an edge in the fight game over their Anglo-Saxon neighbours. He puts it down to their passion.

Although Eddie Thomas had doubts about boxing, for all his soul-searching he knew that, if he had the chance, he would go back into boxing again. Despite the fact that coal mines he had owned have suffered because of his boxing interests.

"Maybe if I had concentrated a bit more on business I would have been happier with that. I don't know," he reflected, "but all I have achieved in boxing I have enjoyed. I have been proud to be associated with the fighters I trained. They were my own boys."

Right until the end there was no shortage of recruits from the Welsh valleys eager to learn their boxing trade. Thomas would pile up to half a dozen youngsters at a time to take them to boxing tournaments around the country.

His home town, Merthyr Tydfil, he considered a fighting town. His first trainer told him it was the toughest place on earth, rivalled only perhaps by the Bowery in New York. People in Merthyr would fight whether inside or outside the ring. Such communities breed boxers.

Even tragedy cannot keep those involved in the fight game away. Dai Gardiner trained Johnny Owen at his gym in New Tredegar in South Wales, but turned his back on the sport after his death. He knew, though, he had to return.

"Since I was a kid, boxing has been in my blood," he explained. "I needed to come back to prove to myself and my family and for Johnny Owen that I could produce a champion. I have worked damn hard ever since."

Gardiner knows boxing is dangerous. Just as there is danger in a lot of other sports like motor racing and horse racing. A common defence of the sport, although one as Gardiner knows that is fundamentally flawed. Nobody in motor racing or as a jockey is there to inflict punishment on another. Injury is an unfortunate consequence of their sports. Not its *raison d'etre*.

Gardiner believes boxers know what they are doing and accept the hazards. Whether they should be allowed to do so is another matter. The trainer is adamant, though, and explains: "With the boxers, I train them hard and they know the dangers before they start. Nobody makes anybody box."

Young people today are putting needles in their arms and stealing cars. Gardiner believes today's society is bad and boxing keeps youngsters on the straight and narrow. It provides discipline. He has trained hundreds of boxers and not many have gone wrong.

The nature of the sport has changed from when Eddie Thomas was fighting. Now enormous sums can be made and successful boxers are major celebrities whose faces are known worldwide. Yet the pitfalls facing fighters are the same as they have always been. When, long after his retirement from the ring, the legendary heavyweight champion Joe Louis was asked if he regretted missing out on the huge purses then on offer, he answered: "No, it would have just been bigger bets."

Efforts are being made to break a cycle as old as the fight game itself. Barry McGuigan has a new role as president of the Professional Boxers' Association, and says: "The vast majority of boxers come from poor backgrounds. When it comes to planning their future, it normally goes wrong for them."

The PBA is tackling the problem, but it is a slow process. It is promoting an adult education programme offering 150 subjects that can be studied so that there is something for the boxer to fall back on at the end of his career. McGuigan believes boxers are still being exploited and need protection.

He is aware of the difficulties. Boxing is a very seductive profession for those who make it to the top. It can be very humiliating to return to being an ordinary member of the public. Boxers miss the money and the quality of life their fists have brought.

Leading managers, as might be expected, take a different view of the fight game and the way fighters are treated. Alex Morrison, a Glasgow manager and promoter, prefers his boxers to keep their day jobs. Although he is aware that criticism is frequently levelled at his side of the fight business, he blames the boxers themselves for most of their problems.

"They always think there will be another pay day tomorrow," he says. "They never believe the money will dry up. Also, many of them live in a dual world. There is the real world of trying to get on in boxing. Then there is the fantasy world of big title matches and money pouring in. Boxers are their own worst enemies."

His fellow Glasgow promoter and manager, Tommy Gilmore, is the third generation of his family in the business. He believes that while in the past boxers lost their money, it was frequently because the managers themselves were poor at planning for the future.

His father and grandfather may have known far more about boxing than himself, but he is more aware of pensions and money management. All his boxers have independent financial advice and are told to invest in pensions. If they become successful an accountant is found for them.

"I am still on friendly terms with every fighter I have ever been involved with," he says. "We have a business to operate, but the boxers are essential to that. The people who come to me are brought by former boxers who know I looked after them. We have a family-type atmosphere here."

While in the past, some managers and promoters may have had a bad reputation, Gilmore believes times have changed and there has been an evolution in the fight game. "Most people involved are in it for the love of boxing."

It all sounds seductive, but Ken Buchanan, the former World lightweight champion, is unlikely to be too impressed. He is still convinced fighters are underpaid and exploited by promoters and managers.

Certainly the history of the Celtic fighters through the years would confirm Buchanan's view. Now, though, with satellite television generating such large purses, perhaps times are changing. If those who give sweat and blood in the hardest of sports actually get to keep the fruits of their labour, then it would not be a moment too soon. Sadly, Eddie Thomas will not be around to see it.

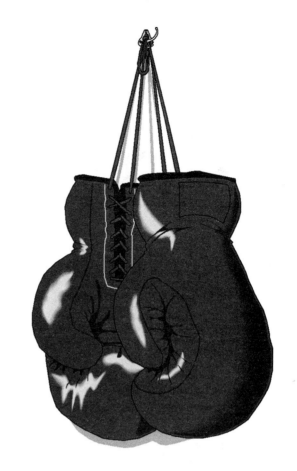

Chapter One

In The Beginning

LONG before they fought for fame and prize-money in the ring, the Celts enjoyed a reputation for being ready to fight whenever pride or honour was at stake.

Early Irish literature portrayed the natives as a physically strong people with a deep love of sport and outdoor activities. The mythical warrior Cuchulainn was supposedly so agile and powerful that he was designated the best all-round athlete in the Gaelic world.

From 632BC to 1169AD, a spectacular festival was held periodically about ten miles from Tara, on the site of the tomb of Tailte, an Irish queen. It was known as the Tailteann Games and huge crowds flocked to enjoy the feats of strength, skill and endurance in sports that included boxing.

Fist-fighting as a sport, however, largely died out until its revival in England in the early 18th century. Like Greece and Rome before it, England at the time considered sport an honourable, even a noble pursuit.

Boxing grew out of its association with sword and cudgel fighting to become recognised as a sport in its own right. However, the sport of boxing was hardly the sport we know today, with wrestling, choking and gouging an integral part of the game.

In Ireland there is evidence that boxing had its roots in the phenomenon of faction fighting. This popular pastime was chiefly practised in rural areas around market days and fairs.

Faction fighting was not a sport but a way of sorting out family rows, disputes over land, or whatever grievances lingered between the rival groups. Death and maiming were very often the grim outcome of faction fights.

James Figg brought order out of chaos and a small smattering of science to barbarity. He opened an amphitheatre in London dedicated to teaching the 'manly arts of foul play, backsword, cudgelling and boxing'.

From the day it opened in 1719, it was patronised by many royal and noble personages — the Fancy - who supported Figg's exhibits with their presence.

As the popularity of boxing grew throughout England in the 18th century, the prize money increased together with the size of the crowds of spectators. In the early days of prize fighting in England, names like Corcoran, Ryan and O'Donnell figured among those who participated.

Perhaps it was their way of articulating their sense of grievance at the centuries of oppression by the English in Ireland, Scotland and Wales. More likely it was the prospect of getting paid for something they liked doing that attracted them to the sport.

The British Isles in general and Ireland in particular have never been over blessed with good heavyweight boxers. The

physical make-up of the Celt tends to mitigate against producing men of the size to win the World crown in the highest
division.

Yet in the early days of the fight game, Ireland did manage
a heavyweight champion and he achieved the distinction in
quick fashion. If the early days, bare-knuckle bouts were apt
to be long, drawn-out affairs as fighters battled to knock
each other senseless, it was certainly not the case when Peter
Corcoran challenged Bill Darts for the title.

Corcoran knocked-out his opponent with one punch in
less than a minute in 1771, although in the murky world of
pugilism of the time there were doubts about how genuine a
contest it had been. The Irishman's backer and fellow
countryman, Colonel O'Kelly, had arranged the bout and
backed heavily on the outcome.

However, for five years the courageous Corcoran was
generally regarded as the British champion. He had beaten
the best-known names around, although there were also
question marks against some of these contests.

Corcoran lost his title in October 1776, at the Crown Inn,
Staines, near London, to Harry Sellers, a West Countryman
who had boxed at the famous Bristol School established by
one of the great pugilists of the era, Jack Slack. There were
again concerns about the legitimacy of the contest with
claims the Irishman had thrown the fight.

It was a sad end to a man who claimed a first for his
country. In a scenario to be repeated through the history of
the fight game, he quickly lost the money he had won and
the admirers from his boxing days faded away. The life of the
first Irishman to be crowned champion of England ended in
a pauper's grave.

If the first Irish champion had won his title quickly, his

countryman, Simon Byrne, earned himself a niche in boxing history in 1833 when his unsuccessful bid to wrest the English heavyweight championship from James 'Deaf' Burke, another son of Irish settlers, lasted for three hours and 16 minutes.

The 99-round contest is the longest championship fight in history, either with bare-knuckles or gloves. The effort cost Byrne his life.

It was a fateful end to the Irishman's career, for three years earlier he had dealt out such a beating to Sandy McKay that the latter failed to recover consciousness and Byrne was put on trial for manslaughter. He was acquitted.

Byrne never trained for lengthy fights. Most of his preparation for a bout involved discussing it with his friends in various taverns throughout Ireland and England. Although he stood 6ft 1in, his 13st 8lbs was mostly positioned around his waistline.

When the championship bout was scheduled for Ascot Racecourse, Byrne asked Ned Neale, a former prominent pugilist, to help him get into trim.

The Irishman's main plan of campaign was to rush Burke to the corner and hold him by the neck with his left hand while belting him with his right.

This tactic proved successful until the 19th round when he damaged his right hand. His chief weapon had now gone. In the 93rd round, Byrne was knocked over by the sheer weight of punches from the champion and was barely able to stand during the following rounds.

Yet he held his ground while trying to keep his opponent at bay with his one good hand. Finally, even his great spirit reached its limit and he collapsed in a heap at Burke's feet.

After being carried unconscious from the ring, Byrne was

put to the surgeon to be surgically bled. The left side of his head was badly bruised, his left eye was completely closed and his mouth and face much swollen. His body also bore many bruises.

The following day his condition worsened. His head was shaved and leeches applied to the bruised parts. He recovered sufficiently to thank those who were attending him, but then suffered a relapse and died.

At the inquest into his death some witnesses deplored the fact that fighters were often carried to the 'scratch' when they could not make it alone. The coroner recorded a verdict of manslaughter against Burke.

He stood trial at Hereford assizes and was found not guilty. Byrne, only 32 when he died, was buried at St Albans in Hertfordshire; a public appeal raised £262 for his widow.

The Irish, shocked at the death of their championship hope, vowed to avenge Byrne's death by finding an Irishman who would relieve Burke of the title.

A candidate was soon found in Samuel O'Rourke. His backers sent over a challenge to stage the fight in Ireland, but in view of the backlash against the champion following Byrne's death, he not surprisingly turned down the invitation.

Events in England had helped focus Irish minds on the United States, where the attraction of prize fighting was beginning to gain support. The cream of Britain and Ireland's talent took ship and went. Almost overnight England was forced to yield its hold on the sport.

Mel Christle, president of the Boxing Union of Ireland, explains that it was Byrne's superhuman effort and the ultimate price he paid for making it that changed the course of fight history. From now on, Irish fighters figure strongly in the boxing records of the United States.

Christle said: "It was the beginning of the end of England as the centre of the universe as far as boxing is concerned."

Irish fighters saw America as a land of opportunity, particularly because a colour bar meant there were no championship bouts against coloured fighters, which made life easier for the Irish.

"The emigration of Irish fighters which began at this time continues," says Christle, "and it is pertinent to emphasis that Ireland is still a major source of professional fighters either those of Irish descent or home-ground boxers who travel abroad to train and ply their trade. It is amazing where these Irish pugilists turn up."

It was in America, in New Orleans, that O'Rourke finally caught up with Burke in one of those contests that served only to lend valuable ammunition to the opponents of boxing.

O'Rourke, a gambler and gangster, had his followers cut the ropes and attack Burke within three rounds of the contest starting, and the ensuing struggle between rival supporters saw firearms used. The two never met in the ring again. O'Rourke's end would come violently. He was discovered murdered at a lumber camp.

Having taken advantage of the situation in England, the New World was quick to take control and it is the United States that has enjoyed world ascendancy over ring affairs ever since.

Bare-knuckle boxing began to establish its roots on American soil around 1830. The New World offered plenty of opportunities to hardy young men with surplus energy to burn and a yearning for fame and fortune.

The ring could provide a short-cut to the goal that motivated many an Irishman fleeing from the famine and deprivation of his homeland. To those with talent in their fists England was no longer the place to look to.

Before the Irish invasion, boxing in the United States had been largely confined to matches between black slaves forced to fight each other for the entertainment of their white masters, who had been introduced to pugilism in England.

It was the tensions between the natives and the Irish immigrants in American cities in the 19th century that established the Celts as the great boxing breed. In many of the early contests it was the custom to have a native American pitted against an Irish fighter to raise public interest.

The potato famine and the brutal policies of landlords had squeezed the poor of Ireland off the land and sent a wave of unskilled peasants towards the large cities of the American north-east. The brutality displayed by the Irish in the ring was symptomatic of the violence endemic to working-class life.

Unemployment and poverty were constant threats. The powerlessness was combined with the occupational hazards that hit the working class with unrivalled force. Staggering numbers of men were killed or maimed on the job.

Indeed, by 1860 there were four Irish women for every three Irish men in New York City, partly because of desertions, partly by the need of breadwinners' to travel in search of work, but also as a result of the high, job-related mortality rates.

In addition, poor diet, overcrowding and lack of modern sanitation contributed to waves of deadly epidemics. The poor lived as their ancestors had, in a world that did little to shield them from pain.

When bare-fist boxing began to be promoted in America,

it was the Irish who took most readily to it. The Irish faced bigotry, with signs warning them away from jobs and accommodation. They rightly felt they were regarded as an under-class.

The United States was also perceived as an 'English' country and boxing provided a chance to fight back. As has proved the case down the years, poverty provided the spur for pugilists.

The late Nat Fleischer, founder and editor of *The Ring* magazine, remarked that the history of the American ring from the middle of the 19th century through the early part of the 20th century, was primarily a source of Irish supremacy.

However, there was a social stigma against boxing in the public eye. Most fighters came from lower-class Irish backgrounds and were ill-educated.

A few fighters, though, not only managed to win a few pounds for their trouble but also gained status. John Morrissey was born in County Tipperary in 1831 and at the age of three travelled to New York with his parents.

Morrissey's ring career culminated in winning the American championship when he defeated John C. Heenan at Long Point, Canada, on 20 October 1858. Heenan's cause was not helped when he injured his right hand after striking a stake in a neutral corner.

After retiring, Morrissey went on to become a leading figure in Irish-American politics as well as operating successful gambling houses. He served two terms in the US Congress.

But it was the charisma of one man which was to win for boxing popular appeal and lift the sport from the illegal, socially unacceptable status it held until his arrival. On both sides of the Atlantic the sport was in danger of falling into disrepute and its practitioners were being harried by the authorities.

John L. Sullivan is generally recognised as the first-ever World heavyweight champion. He was also probably the first sports superstar. And he gave boxing a mass appeal it still enjoys.

The 'Boston Strong Boy' was born in 1858 and dominated the boxing world in the latter half of the 19th century. His father was from Tralee, County Clare, and his mother from Athlone, County Westmeath.

He had watched his father work doggedly to keep the family barely above poverty. A few early fights in Boston theatres kindled in John L. Sullivan a taste for fame and adulation that the workaday could never satisfy. Few Irish immigrants could have resisted the glory, the money and the peer approval that the sport offered.

He would fight anyone, anywhere, with bare fists, skin-tight or padded gloves, under any rules. He advertised in the newspapers: 'I will fight any man breathing. Always on the level, yours truly, John L. Sullivan.'

Another method of drumming up business was less refined. He would issue a challenge to anyone in a pub or tavern with the boast: "I'll lick any son of a bitch in the house." His temper was notorious, but his followers idolised him.

His tour offering $1,000 to any man who could go four rounds with him in a gloved contest helped make the sport popular with the working class. His journeys around the country also included bouts with the best fighters around.

Sullivan's assets were speed and non-stop aggression. As an athlete he had been good enough to attract the attention of professional baseball clubs. He would fight any white fighter.

It is to his disgrace that he would not fight any of the talented black boxers who were his contemporaries. In particular, Peter Jackson, who was thought by many to be the best at that time. Sullivan's decision not to fight him on grounds of race owed much to a fear that he would be beaten.

In May 1881, Sullivan fought John 'the Bull's Head Terror' Flood on a moonlit barge towed a few miles up the Hudson River, outside the jurisdiction of the New York City police.

The match was fought with skin-tight gloves in front of the usual crowd of working-class men, urban dandies, and professional gamblers. Sullivan easily won the 15-minute fight by knocking or throwing down his opponent in each of the eight rounds.

This led to a championship fight with Paddy Ryan, born in Thurles, County Tipperary, in 1853. Ryan had won the championship in his first professional contest from the 42-year-old Joe Goss in 1880 at Colliers Station, West Virginia, in an 86-round contest.

Two years later, backers of John L. Sullivan issued a challenge for the title and a fight was arranged in Mississippi City where Ryan was stopped in the ninth round. Ryan had achieved the unique record of winning a title in his first pro fight and losing it in his second.

In an international contest Sullivan faced the Englishman Charlie Mitchell, on the estate of Baron Rothschild near Chantilly, France, on 10 March 1888. Pre-fight preparations included a man with a revolver in each pocket warning that there would be fair play from the largely British supporters certain to favour their man.

The fighters themselves had soaked their fists in walnut juice and wore spikes on their shoes. If fair play from the crowd had been assured, it was not so with the boxers, Mitchell at one point sticking the spike of his boot into Sullivan's leg.

The cloying mud made boxing difficult.

When the action was brought to a close after 39 rounds, both sides claimed their man had had the better of the proceedings. Heavy rain had made conditions treacherous and it was the decision of the seconds that the contest should be called to a halt and the match declared a draw.

As they made to leave the police arrived. As in England, boxing in France was illegal and the two fighters found themselves imprisoned. Sullivan was released on bail and caught a ship home. A 2,000 franc fine imposed later in his absence remained unpaid.

The following year, Sullivan signed to fight John K. Kilrain, who also claimed to be the World bare-knuckle champion. The match was made to decide who was truly the best boxer in the world. Because boxing was at this time illegal in all 38 states of the USA, the fight took place 200 miles outside New Orleans.

After fighting for two hours and 16 minutes in 104 degree heat, Kilrain quit in the 76th round — and John L. Sullivan was the first undisputed World heavyweight champion. The contest was the last heavyweight championship fight held under London Prize Ring rules.

In 1866, the Marquess of Queensberry laid down a set of rules for glove-fighting upon which boxing as we know it today is founded. The pioneer work was done: the sport was given a new order and cleaned up.

It was presented to the public as a trial of strength and

skill within decent limits, rather than as a hideous duel with fists which could never be settled until one man had been battered senseless.

Unlike the old London Prize Ring Rules, gloves were to be worn. And there were other difference which changed the whole nature of the contest. There was now a duration of rounds rather than the old fight to the finish. Boxers also now had ten seconds, rather than 30, to recover from a knock down. And wrestling was not allowed.

Sullivan did not fight again for three years, during which time a new challenger emerged. Jim Corbett lived in San Francisco although his father was from Tuam, County Galway, and his mother from Dublin.

Corbett and Sullivan agreed to fight under the Queensberry Rules using 5oz boxing gloves. This was to be the first heavyweight championship fight under the new regulations. The stakes were $20,000 with a purse of $25,000.

Sullivan was out of training and out of condition. His weight had soared. Apart from a few exhibition bouts, he had not thrown a punch in anger in three years. Most of his energies had gone into his stage performances as the hero of a melodrama entitled *Honest Hearts and Willing Hands*.

Lack of fitness and over-confidence were to be the champion's undoing. Although Sullivan was a strong favourite and heavily outweighed his opponent, he was unable to land the booming right hand that ended so many of his earlier contests.

Corbett, wily and quick, was not an opponent of the old toe-to-toe school. He eventually knocked-out a weary Sullivan in 21 rounds and the reign of John L. was over. His supporters could not believe the era of their great champion had ended.

John L. Sullivan's official record shows he won 38 out of his 42 fights with three drawn, and only once was he knocked-out. Although more a bruiser than a scientific boxer, he was a stout-hearted fighter who fought the best white fighters around.

On his retirement Sullivan exchanged the ring for the stage and went on to lecture on the virtues of prohibition. Rare archive footage shows a grey, overweight avuncular figure being introduced to a crowd before a fight and throwing a few gentle sparring punches at the contenders.

Gentleman Jim Corbett, having disposed of a legend, found the public unforgiving. Yet the former bank clerk brought to the sport a respectability which it had lacked hitherto. Like his predecessor he also took to the stage.

While for the modern-day fighter there are game shows and TV quizzes to cash in on their fame, the Victorian equivalent was the stage and vaudeville allied to exhibition bouts.

Boxers appeared as the main character in dramas written especially for them. British heavyweight Frank Bruno's stage pantomime performances in recent times are certainly nothing new.

Corbett enjoyed the life and in 1894 retired from the ring.

His choice of successor was another leading Irish fighter who was a heavyweight contender in the years before the new century. Peter Maher was born in Galway and began his professional boxing career in 1888.

Maher's main claim to fame was in the first 'filmed fight that never was'. His opponent was the Englishman Bob Fitzsimmons, who had already defeated him with a 12th-round knock-out in their first fight although a spirited performance by Maher had troubled the experienced Fitzsimmons.

Their second encounter was for the heavyweight title vacated since Corbett's retirement. Although Corbett had announced that he had turned his crown over to Maher as his natural successor, there was little public backing for the move.

Fitzsimmons also disputed the claim and so they met in an open-air contest in Texas which was to have been the first boxing match filmed for a motion picture.

Fitzsimmons was said to have been unhappy with his money for the film rights and whether that was a factor is unknown, but he knocked-out Maher in the first round before the cameras had chance to roll. It was to be Maher's last championship chance in a career that ended with his retirement in 1908.

Corbett returned and had been World champion for five years before losing his crown to Fitzsimmons. The fight was held in Carson City, Nevada, on 17 March, St Patrick's Day, 1897, in a contest captured on film. The archive footage survives and was given a special showing in London to mark the centenary of the fight.

Sheriff Bat Masterson stood at the entrance and collected 400 guns from the paying customers. Another lawman, Marshal Wyatt Earp, stood in Corbett's corner with a six-shooter for protection.

Corbett had his opponent on the canvas in the sixth round and was having by far the better of the exchanges against Fitzsimmons, who struggled to land a knock-out blow that would end the contest.

It is said that encouragement from his wife Rose at ringside played a part in the Englishman's triumph with the cry: "Hit him in the slats [ribs], Bob," which encouraged her husband to switch his attack to the body of Corbett. In the 13th round a blow to the solar plexus ended the fight.

Fitzsimmons was born the son of a blacksmith in Helston, Cornwall, where the Celtic influence is still strong. Attempts to revive the ancient Cornish culture and language are backed by their Celtic relations in Wales, and Welsh nationalists help their counterparts in Cornwall.

Whether Fitzsimmons considered himself a Celt is not known, but he certainly had Irish ancestors which gave him red colouring and earned him the monicker 'Ruby Bob'. By his 20s he was going bald and had freckles. His fight record also would not disgrace anyone from the Celtic nations.

He was the first man to win three World titles. Others have matched the numbers but none will emulate the divisions he triumphed in, winning the middleweight, light-heavyweight and heavyweight titles. Until the modern era and the variety of governing bodies, he was the only British World heavyweight champion.

Fitzsimmons was regarded as a physical freak with thin legs but a powerful upper body honed in his occupation as a blacksmith. He was also said to be able to shift his weight between 160lbs and 200lbs within a matter of weeks and without it affecting his fighting prowess. What he lacked in skill he made up for in punching power and durability. He was also remarkable for the longevity of his career. He did not finally retire until 1914 at the age of 52.

Another Irish heavyweight making his mark at this time was former sailor Tom Sharkey, easily recognisable with his cauliflower ear and star and ship tattoo on his chest. He fought a gruelling 25-round contest with champion Jim Jeffries for the heavyweight crown.

Sharkey had already fought and beaten Fitzsimmons in 1896 when the Cornishman was ruled to have unleashed a foul blow. The decision in the eighth round was delivered by the famous gunfighting marshal Wyatt Earp, but was considered a travesty.

Before the fight, rumour was rife that a large gambling syndicate had bet heavily on Sharkey and the contest was fixed. The Fitzsimmons camp was unhappy, but there was little they could do and it was thought a knock-out would remove any chance of a dubious decision. They were wrong.

When the two fought again in a properly supervised contest, Fitzsimmons got his revenge and a second chance to win the title he had lost to James J. Jeffries. The blacksmith's son from Cornwall lost in 1902 against a champion 11 years younger and 38lbs heavier, who absorbed all the punishment he could throw.

It gave Sharkey his opportunity with the champion. The bout, fought in Coney Island, New York, was the second time the two had met, with Jeffries already having won a non-title bout over 20 rounds.

Their latest encounter was also the first filmed under artificial lights which, added to the heat of the day, made it a draining experience for both fighters.

It was a terrific battle in which, despite sustaining two broken ribs, Sharkey put up a tremendous fight. When it was over and Jeffries had retained his title on a points decision, the Irishman repaired to hospital for treatment.

The two were to enact this famous battle as a vaudeville act in the 1920s with two balding and overweight figures going through the motions of the fight.

While the heavyweight division then, as now, was the most glamorous and attracted by far the most attention, there was Irish involvement in the lighter divisions. Here again native or second generation Irish fighters excelled. One of the most distinguished names in the sport is that of Jack Dempsey.

Boxing history has produced two Jack Dempseys, each of them an outstanding World champion. Yet in neither case was Jack Dempsey his real name.

Mention of the name to most fight fans immediately brings to mind the great heavyweight who was World champion from 1919 to 1926. This William Harrison Dempsey adopted the name in honour of the Irishman who was the first holder of the World middleweight title.

To distinguish between the two, the original Jack Dempsey is given the prefix 'Nonpareil', the unrivalled or incomparable. He was born Jack Kelly, near Clane, County Kildare, in 1862, and was taken to America as a child.

The family settled in the Brooklyn district of New York. When he started boxing, Kelly took the name Jack Dempsey to spare his family's feelings as they had no great love for the sport.

Dempsey fought in the era that bridged both bare-knuckle and gloved combat. He started out as a wrestler but soon laid claim to the World middleweight boxing crown after beating the Canadian, George Fulljames, at Staten Island, in 1884.

He made a series of successful defences until failing health threatened his career. He was tempted to take one more fight by a $12,000 purse.

His opponent was Bob Fitzsimmons, who was later to relieve Corbett of his heavyweight crown. Dempsey was hammered to defeat in 15 rounds.

It was nearly the end of the road for one of the great Irish fighters. His last ring appearance was in an exhibition bout with John L. Sullivan. It was a benefit show for Dempsey, short of cash and in poor health. Within five months of that fight he was dead, a victim of tuberculosis, aged 33.

In the lightweight division few can match the record of Jack McAuliffe, from Cork, Ireland, who retired undefeated after having fought in both the bare-knuckle and gloved era.

A career that started in 1884 in New York, when he was 18, saw him fight for 11 years through to his last title defence in New Orleans in 1892. Before his fight for the World crown, he won what was regarded as the American title from Jack Hopper.

The World title fight on November 5, 1887, in Revere, near Boston, Massachusetts, was at a time when boxing was illegal and the authorities were keen to clamp down. It was held in a stable with guests being taken in pairs from a nearby hotel to the venue while a Salvation Army choir sang hymns to fool the police.

McAuliffe's opponent was the British champion, Jem Carney, and the two fought a brutal 74 rounds before an invasion of the ring by spectators who had bet on the Irishman forced the referee to call a halt and the contest was declared a draw.

Although boxing was still in many ways at an early stage of development, the sport which had started 180 years before on a wooden stage at James Figg's amphitheatre, ended by the turn of the century with boxing being the first truly global sport.

From its grotesque origins it had acquired a state of some respectability as pictures of the ranks of dinner-jacketed spectators watching bouts at the National Sporting Club in London testify.

Boxing did not just reflect the bloodiness of life. Rather it helped shape violence into art, bringing order and meaning. At its best the ring rendered mayhem rule-bound instead of anarchic, voluntary rather than random.

Despite the brutality of their trade, boxers made bloodshed comprehensible and thus offered models of honourable conduct. They taught men to face danger with courage, to be impervious to pain, and to return violence rather than passively accept it.

Chapter Two

On the Home Front

W HILE America may have established itself as the
world centre of the fight game, the sport on the
home front continued to flourish.

Boxing had established its classic headquarters in London. The National Sporting Club was a little building in Covent Garden where a full house of 1,300 members could witness a programme built up from the finest exponents of skill and stamina in the land.

Next to the establishment of the club, the revival of boxing in Britain and Ireland owed much to the provision, in 1909, of the Championship Challenge Belts offered by Lord Lonsdale for competition at fixed weights.

With more money coming into the sport and the arrival of promoters with a business background keen to cash in, there was a growth in fight venues where boxers could ply their trade.

The old hard-bitten, all-weather sport did not change overnight, however. The rarefied atmosphere of the National Sporting Club, where men 'boxed' and the word 'fight' was never used, would have been altogether too refined for patrons who had only just turned their backs on the old Prize Ring.

The sport might have its headquarters, but it could only prosper if it appealed to the common masses. Boxing flourished in the fairground booths with the owner of the booth travelling with his stable of boxers who would take on all-comers for money. The fairground produced some of the finest boxers the world has seen.

Popular destinations for the booths included the Scottish Highlands, the industrial valleys of South Wales and the market towns of Ireland.

Frankie O'Donnell, secretary of the Scottish Ex-Boxers' Association, recalls the booth days and the peculiar skills they demanded of the boxers who earned £7 a week, three times the average weekly wage for a working man.

He explained: "Booth fighting was very successful throughout most of Britain. The big Scottish cities had permanent booths and for the boxers it was a way of making extra money. Most boxed under a different name."

Some boxers would be placed in the crowd to volunteer when the barker called for anyone to take on the booth boxers on the rostrum. It was a good way of drumming up trade.

O'Donnell said the fighters could take on three fights a day, although some of the contests would be mock bouts against boxers they knew. Such shows were known as 'gee' fights in the trade. If it was a genuine volunteer' he would get paid for each round he survived and could win more than a week's wage if he lasted the three rounds.

Iori Davies joined a booth in the 1930s in his native South Wales when he challenged the booth champion and won. He had the advantage of watching the champion fight a few bouts and knew there were weaknesses that could be exploited.

And Davies was no street fighter fancying his chances on a Saturday night after a few pints in the pub. He was a keen boxer looking for a professional career in the fight game and his trainer had recommended the booths as a good learning ground.

After winning the fight with the champion in the second round, Davies was asked by the proprietor if he wanted to join. He accepted and has no regrets. Summers were spent touring from fair to fair throughout England and Wales and although he also boxed as a professional, his booth days were the most enjoyable.

"You never knew who was going to take up the challenge," he said. "Drunks who liked to scrap were no problem. If we were busy I would sometimes take on two at a time over the three rounds. I also had to fight men much heavier, but I was never seriously hurt."

He remembers a man emerging from the crowd who looked as though he could handle himself. The booth proprietor warned him that his opponent looked useful and to be careful. It was a hell of a scrap and the challenger stayed on his feet the three rounds to collect his money. It emerged that he was the Scottish welterweight champion.

Davies said many of the leading boxers joined the booths because it was good experience as well as for the money. Having so many fights sharpened technique and ensured that fitness levels were high.

It was from this boxing booth tradition in the early years of the new century, up to and including World War One, that many great boxers were to emerge, including two Scots who were to make a huge impression.

The boxing rivalry between Edinburgh and Glasgow is deeply rooted in pugilistic history. The common conception north and south of the border is that, without question, Glasgow is and always has been Scotland's first city of fisticuffs.

Glasgow may win on the number of boxers produced. And promoters used to testify that Edinburgh is a financial graveyard for boxing matches. Yet the first Scots to win an Olympic medal and a Lonsdale Belt respectively were East Coast men.

Despite attempts by the Glasgow-dominated Olympic Selection Committee to exclude him, High Roddin, of Musselburgh, won Scotland's first-ever Olympic boxing medal at the 1908 London games.

James 'Tancy' Lee of Leith became Scotland's first-ever Lonsdale Belt winner, defeating the legendary Jimmy Wilde at the National Sporting Club in January 1915.

Roddin was born of Irish-Catholic parents in the Newbigging district of Musselburgh. Raised as a devout son of the Roman Catholic faith, there were family hopes that he would enter the priesthood. Such aspirations did not long survive his meeting with Charlie Cotter. From 1895, when he established his gym at 84 Leith Street, until the advent of Nat Dresner in 1922, Cotter dominated Scottish boxing.

Cotter was a man of many parts. He had acted as time-keeper at one of the last bare-knuckle contests held in Scotland, at Roslin, on the outskirts of Edinburgh.

In direct contrast to his participation in this blatantly unlawful activity, Cotter was also a renowned physical trainer of the ultra-respectable Scottish aristocracy and upper middle classes.

Advocates, aristocrats and city merchants came under Cotter's tutelage at his 'Eleven O'Clock Club,' so-called because this was the appointed hour of the evening that they came together.

Roddin had thus entrusted his fistic future to a man of impeccable fighting pedigree. Following his victory at the Scottish amateur championships, Roddin assumed he would be on the way to the fourth Olympic games in London.

However, not for the first or last time was a boxer to discover that administrative politics could provide a bigger challenge to his fistic ambitions than any opponent inside the ring.

When the ruling body, the Scottish Gymnastics Association, announced their original Olympic choices, there was an uproar. Only three boxers were selected and they were all from the one club, The National in Glasgow.

The Eastern clubs protested so vehemently that the Glasgow faction agreed to add two more names to the squad, Paddy Fee and Hugh Roddin. The latter went on to win a bronze medal.

For the majority of young working-class men in 1908, long hours of monotonous toil for low pay was the harsh daily reality. Little wonder, then, that within a year of his Olympic triumph Hughie Roddin had turned professional, marking his debut in the paid ranks by beating Harry Thomas in Leith Drill Hall.

In his second fight Roddin's path crossed with one of the world's great boxers, Jim Driscoll. Peerless Jim had watched the young Scot prior to his own contest and had complimented Roddin on his performance. With new-found confidence, Roddin decided to forsake the shores of the Firth of Forth for those of the United States.

He set sail for New York City in February 1911. In the
1890s one of the top boxing centres in New York had been
the Scottish American Athletic Club and Roddin attracted a
cult following of Scots emigrants throughout his American
tour.

He was made a life member of the city's famous 'Acme'
boxing club and was presented with a gold watch and chain
bought with funds raised on his behalf by club members.

There were also disappointments to be endured,
primarily his failure to land a fight with the reigning Scottish
bantamweight champion, his arch rival Alex Lafferty of
Airdrie, who was also fighting out of New York.

They had met socially, but were fated never to meet in the
ring. Lafferty spent most of 1913 touring Wales, England
and Ireland. The first six months of 1914 were spent in New
York before the outbreak of World War One. One of the many
casualties of Ludendorff's spring offensive in 1918 was Sgt
Alex Lafferty of the Royal Engineers.

Tancy Lee had not started out on his professional career
until he was 28, making his achievement in winning a
Lonsdale Belt outright all the more remarkable, particularly
as he was fighting at a time when there were a lot of good
boxers around in the lighter divisions.

He won a flyweight title fight with Jimmy Wilde, but held
the title for only nine months before losing to Joe Symonds.
In a return with Wilde, the Welshman had his revenge. At 34,
an age when most boxers are slipping into retirement, he
won three victories in the space of 15 months to make the
featherweight belt his own. He boxed on until he was in his
40s.

If Scotland was proving fertile for boxing talent, the
industrial valleys of South Wales were to prove more than a

CELTIC FISTS

match. The Rhondda Valley was a name that became known around the world: it was a place were work could be had and, it was said, fortunes could be made. It attracted both the rural Welsh and swarms of immigrant workers.

Thousands settled along the River Taff and the Glamorgan Canal which carried iron from Merthyr down to the sea at Cardiff. There was work, but no streets paved with gold. People were exploited and condemned to a miserable existence. Many had to endure squalid conditions with infant mortality of such huge proportions that a child was lucky to survive five years.

One of Merthyr's boxing legends, the late Eddie Thomas, a British and European welterweight champion who managed two World champions, spoke of children coming so angrily into the world that their fists were already clenched.

In that setting, those that survived were quick to use those fists. Thomas recalled that arguments were settled out on the coal tips with an eager crowd looking on. For boys and young men sent down the mines and expected to work long hours for little pay, there had to be a release. Fighting was one outlet for their frustration.

In a town that then boasted more than 160 public houses, a fight could be guaranteed outside every one on a Saturday night as drunken men poured out. Thomas said that bandits and rogues flourished. It was, he believed, the toughest place on earth apart from perhaps the notorious Bowery in New York.

Yet the community spirit that epitomises valleys towns like Merthyr was forged from such adverse social conditions and an atmosphere of violence fuelled in part by resentment and jealousy between immigrants and the Welsh natives.

Thomas remembered that it was not just boxers who

flourished. Within a stone's throw of where he was raised, four composers were born who between them contributed 88 hymns to the Welsh hymn book.

Two of the three great fighters of this era were to emerge from this industrial hell-hole that had replaced the small village communities of the mid-19th century. Jim Driscoll and Jimmy Wilde achieved a status in their sport still remembered and lauded today.

A third valleys fighter was to complete the trio — and win a World title — from a more privileged background. Freddie Welsh was that rarity in boxing circles. A well-to-do man from a middle-class family who developed a love of boxing backed by considerable talent.

However, in the roll call of honour of Welsh boxers from this time, two others were to produce performances that gives them an important footnote among the chapters generated by the genius of Driscoll, Wilde and Welsh.

The first was a farmer's son from Cardigan, Tom Thomas. The family moved to Carncelyn Farm in the Rhondda Valley when Tom was a boy. It was an isolated existence and Thomas became obsessed with boxing after a visit to a travelling booth.

The farm barn became his gym, but there were no sparring partners for him to box with, so he practised his skills with his friend and enemy, a bull by the name of Billy One-Horn.

Thomas engaged in round after round of man-to-animal combat, the boxer firing out straight lefts and right crosses at the animal's forehead with sufficient power to punch himself out of danger.

The workout was obviously effective. Thomas joined Jack Scarrott's booth and at the age of 29 went on to win the

British middleweight crown, picking up the second-ever Lonsdale Belt for his efforts after his countryman Welsh had secured the first.

He went into the title fight against Charlie Wilson in December 1909 unbeaten in some 40 professional fights and with a reputation as a hard puncher. Thomas knocked-out his opponent in the second round.

Throughout his career, though, Thomas was crippled with rheumatic fever which some blamed on his habit of diving into the ice-cold waters on the farm lake after his training sessions.

One boxing scribe of the day related that, during a meeting with Thomas, the boxer opened up a vein in his forearm, saying: "Watch this." White acid of the illness spurted freely, before being discoloured by the following blood. The illness first robbed him of any chance to go for the World title and later claimed his life. He was 31.

In a short career, Percy Jones had the distinction of becoming Wales's first World champion. From a mining family in Porth, Jones was born in December 1892 and began his professional career as a 19-year-old after winning a competition in his home town. He had idolised Peerless Jim Driscoll and came under the Master's tuition late on in his career. His speed and useful punching power for a man of 8st saw him win his first 27 bouts, including 24 fights crammed into 1913.

It was a sequence that convinced the National Sporting Club that Jones was ready for his most important fight. In London in 1914, he continued his winning streak and won the World, European and British titles from Bill Ladbury in a comfortable points victory.

He enjoyed a quick successful defence before seven weeks later at Plymouth, his unbeaten run ended at the hands of

Joe Symonds, who knocked him out in the 18th round. The National Sporting Club did not recognise the result, but it was a short reprieve.

Because he had come in overweight, his titles were not at stake, but he lost to Tancy Lee in a punishing 14-round contest. His attempt to continue his career in the bantamweight division was thwarted by World War One, for which Jones enlisted in the Royal Welsh Fusiliers and was quickly promoted to sergeant.

In 1916 he received severe leg wounds and was badly affected by poison gas. He underwent 30 operations, including the amputation of a leg in 1918. He became a desperately sad figure towards the end. In June 1922 he made a rare public appearance with Jim Driscoll at a charity function. His weight was down to 4st 2lbs. He was suffering from trench fever and his remaining leg had become infected and he was confined to a wheelchair. He died on Christmas Day 1922, one day short of his 30th birthday.

The Irish immigrants of the mid-19th century established their own community in Cardiff in an area known as 'Irishtown', a huddle of streets between the docks and the railway station. It was here that Jim Driscoll was born in December 1881.

Driscoll's father, a railwayman, was knocked down and killed in the goods yard near their home when Driscoll was only a few months old and his mother Elizabeth was left to raise her four young children on Parish Relief of six shillings a week.

The chairman of the Guardians reduced the allowance to four shillings when he decided that the children were so clean, tidily dressed and well-nourished that their mother must have some hidden source of income.

She was forced to go to work to feed her family, rising at 4.30 every morning to meet trawlers as they docked to buy the fish which she then sold around the streets. When that income proved inadequate, she laboured as a potato loader on England's Wharf, a hard and punishing job normally done by men.

Jim Driscoll was employed as a boy in a newspaper cutting room in Cardiff. He learned to box using wastepaper around his hands and began his fight career travelling in the boxing booth which toured the valleys.

He was toughened by the hard life under the canvas and his skills developed. Stories of his boxing became well enough known to reach the National Sporting Club and he soon became its star attraction.

He was crowned British featherweight champion and then decided to try his luck in the United States. The Americans preferred their own all-action fighters and Driscoll was concerned that they would not pay to watch his technical skills. He need not have worried.

Tales of his boxing ability had preceded him across the Atlantic and the crowds were ready to pay to see the man already dubbed 'peerless' by the American press.

Driscoll proceeded to take on and beat the best fighters the Americans could find, appearing in a string of fights with barely a blow being landed on him. In any comprehensive list of all-time great featherweights, he is included at the very highest echelon.

He lost only three of his 69 fights, yet he was never crowned World champion. The answer as to how he could achieve such legendary status without ever having held the greatest prize of all lies in the age in which he fought.

Peerless Jim flourished during the first decade of the 20th

century which was the hey-day of the no-decision vogue in the United States. Unless one of the boxers was knocked-out, the fight was not adjudicated by the referee and was recorded as a no-decision contest.

The World champion at the time was Abe Attell, from San Francisco, who refused to fight Driscoll outside a no-decision contest. However, it was the practice at the time for journalists covering the fight to give their verdict which was accepted for betting purposes.

When Attell met Driscoll in February 1910, there was a unanimous verdict that the man from Cardiff was the winner. Ring historian Nat Fleischer, commenting on the fight, said: "Once again we have ND against this meeting in the record books, however Driscoll was easily the best. The Welshman easily outpointed Abe Attell and virtually took his World title away from him. He definitely proved, as far as I am concerned, that he was the best featherweight in the world."

Driscoll was offered a return bout against the champion with his title on the line, but before leaving Wales he had promised to return to box an exhibition at the Nazareth House Orphanage annual charity show.

He gave up the chance to claim the title before he would break his word. He sailed for Wales the following day and did not even stay long enough to claim his purse.

"I gave the sisters of Nazareth House my promise that I would appear there on St David's Day," he explained, "and I never break a promise."

The Welsh welcomed him home as World champion anyway and when his carriage was drawn through the streets of Cardiff on his return, the police were out in force to control the huge crowds that had gathered.

His gesture and the publicity it attracted helped to raise more than £6,000 for the orphanage. For his part the boxer cherished the scroll presented to him by the nuns in recognition of his efforts for them.

It read: 'We can never forget, sir, how in the very zenith of your success, when the fame of your prowess was on every tongue, you generously sacrificed pecuniary advantage and undertook a voyage of some thousands of miles in order to fulfil your promise of assisting Nazareth House.

'Our earnest prayers are that He who never forgets a service done in His name, who promises a reward to those who aid even the least of His little ones, may grant you all the temporal blessings in this world and an imperishable reward hereafter.'

On his return he collected the first-ever Lonsdale Belt after reclaiming the British title, and was then pitched into a big-money grudge match against Freddie Welsh.

The fight was staged in their home city of Cardiff. The two were good friends, although it was said that the pre-match hype was to sour their relationship. The contest itself failed to live up to expectations with Welsh's gift for spoiling tactics and general evasiveness totally nullifying Driscoll's flawless technique.

On several occasions Peerless Jim appealed to the referee to stop Welsh's rough-house tactics, until the tenth round when his patience snapped and he deliberately butted his opponent in the face. Following his disqualification he pleaded for a return but it never materialised. Driscoll's health was now failing, but his supreme boxing skills allowed him to continue way beyond the height of his physical prowess.

Speaking at the Duke of Edinburgh pub which Peerless

Jim bought and which the family have run ever since, Betty Flynn has her own theory about the Welsh fight that seemed to leave such an uncharacteristic blight on his career.

The great niece of the boxer believes that the disqualification controversy had been planned between the two. Her father had told her that the two boxers wanted to find a way of keeping their ring reputations. "It was a put-up job," she claims, "I doubt the butt really hurt him that much."

She added: "They were good friends and there are pictures of them at the races together. They both liked a bet. It was a controversial fight certainly, but not the great rift that people claim between them."

She believes her view is confirmed by the fact that although Peerless Jim lost by disqualification, he still took the larger share of the purse, receiving £1,500 to Welsh's £1,000.

During World War One, Driscoll served as a sergeant-instructor and when the fighting on the battlefields stopped, his battles in the ring continued. He did not really want to fight, but he needed the money.

For one last big pay-day, Driscoll was matched against the man who was probably the best featherweight in the world at the time, Charles Ledoux.

The Frenchman was at his peak and was 11 years younger than Driscoll, who was now a very sick man. Four days before the fight he was confined to his bed with severe stomach pains and he remained there until the morning of the contest. His friends pleaded with him to call it off, but he refused.

The old master climbed into the ring and the crowd gasped. An aged and haggard-looking man, far removed from the boxer in his prime, was about to take on the world's best. Driscoll answered the bell to give what many consider the finest exhibition of classical boxing ever seen in any ring.

For round after round he danced around the bewildered Frenchman, stabbing his gloves effortlessly into his face. Ledoux was unable to land a telling blow and the fight was so one-sided he joined in the applause for the ring genius of Driscoll before returning to his stool at the end of the eighth round.

Although Driscoll was a very sick man in the grip of consumption, he had somehow regained his gift for one last time. It was as if God Himself had decided that Peerless Jim could not go out like ordinary fighters.

By the 15th round, Driscoll was easily ahead on points and a crowd at first fearful for his safety began to hold out hope that he might survive the full 20 and claim victory.

It was not to be. Against a tiring Driscoll, the Frenchman connected with a wild hook to the body which knocked his opponent to the floor and, despite attempts to revive him, the fight was now lost.

It was the end of an illustrious career for Peerless Jim. A collection was taken up for him which raised more than £5,000 before the end of that night's boxing. He returned to the Duke of Edinburgh pub, which had become an informal social centre for the city's war crippled and unemployed, and where few left poorer than when they arrived.

Betty Flynn remembers her father telling stories of that generosity and how he was always willing to help out anyone who needed it. On one occasion he made ten trips to local butchers to buy chickens to give away to the needy at Christmas.

She said: "He was a wonderful man who gave most of his money away. In the end he did not have much, but he had always been kind and wouldn't have wanted it any other way. A lot of people in the area were very poor and life was difficult and Jim knew what that was like."

The illness that had sapped his fighting skills was soon to take his life. He died on 30 January 1925, and the degree of respect and affection which he commanded was underlined when more than 100,000 lined the streets of Cardiff for what was, and still is to this day, the largest funeral seen in Wales.

There was a military escort for the coffin draped in the Union Flag, but the sight that would have undoubtedly pleased Peerless Jim more was the 100 children from Nazareth House Orphanage who led the procession.

The man whose only fault was considered his over generosity and who had been born into the poverty of Irishtown went out as 'The King of Cardiff'. To this day, visitors still call at the pub to look at the large portrait of Jim Driscoll hanging behind the bar and to ask to see the title belts the family still own.

Nowadays the flyweight division is dying out in Western Europe. Better social conditions are breeding sturdier men. The best 'little men' of today come from the Far East or Central America.

However, at the turn of the century, a combination of inadequate diet and hard, bad working conditions was producing an abundance of short, pugnacious men of 8st or less. It used to be said that you only had to whistle down a pit shaft in South Wales and up came a prospective World champion.

When the whistle was answered in 1911, the figure that emerged stood an inch or two over five feet and weighed considerably less than a hundredweight sack of coal which, by curious coincidence, is exactly the 8st weight of a flyweight.

Jimmy Wilde, though, was not to be just a champion; he is hailed by many as the best boxer the division has ever known and lays strong claim to being, pound for pound, the best the British Isles has ever produced.

Among his admirers is Barry McGuigan, the Clones Cyclone who won the World featherweight title more than 70 years later. He described Wilde: "The best British, Irish or Celt boxer ever. He was unique and his style was well before his time."

McGuigan believes that although Wilde was undoubtedly a puncher whose power was produced from unlikely pipe-stem arms, his success owed more than to just being able to deliver a knock-out blow.

His bobbing and weaving style made him a difficult target to hit, but more important was the fact he was the first good combination puncher. While others still threw single shots, the little Welshman would rain a string of blows down on opponents.

Wilde was born in 1892, in the Tylorstown region of Pontypridd where the boys were sent to the collieries as soon as they were old enough.

He turned to boxing to supplement the wages he earned clawing away at the coal-face, where his diminutive size enabled him to crawl into the narrow seams and, legend has it, lying on his back or sides pick away at the face, thus developing the abnormally powerful muscles in his back and shoulders.

Wilde was lodging at the time with David John Davies, known locally as 'Dai the Champion' because of his reputation as a mountain fighter, a peculiar Welsh brand of bare-knuckle fighting practised on mountain sides where crowds could gather away from the prying eyes of the authorities.

Davies found the young Wilde having an argument in his garden with another young miner and ordered them to meet on the mountain at dawn the next morning. There the future World champion broke his rival's jaw in three places and had to contribute most of his meagre earnings to the man's keep during the fortnight in which his injuries kept him away from work.

Jimmy quickly learned that his 5st, 4ft 6ins frame could be exploited to greater effect in the boxing booths than in the narrow seams in which he mined for coal.

Folklore has it that in one morning in Jack Scarrott's booth, Wilde knocked-out 17 opponents, took a ten-minute break for lunch, then returned to knock-out another eight. For flattening 25 opponents in one day he received 15 shillings, a good week's pay in the pit, and decided that boxing was preferable to mining as a living.

His boxing career extended more than 15 years, during which time he won more than 400 fights. His official record shows 153 of them with six defeats, but many of those reversals were to fighters to whom he was conceding a large weight difference.

While the fundamental difficulty for all flyweights reaching maturity is making the weight while retaining enough strength to be able to give of their best, it never proved a problem for Wilde who never fought heavier than 7st 10lbs. Wilde was a physical freak whose skinny legs and thin arms belied considerable punching power. Film footage of his fights shows a curious style with arms held at his waist and constantly attacking. He was nicknamed 'The Ghost with a Hammer in his Hand'.

In a rare reversal, he lost a fight for the British title in 1915 to Tancy Lee, from Leith, the referee stopping the contest in the 17th round. It would be six years before Wilde lost another fight in his own division. The following year Wilde became champion when he knocked-out Joe Symonds in 11 rounds, although the authorities in the United States refused to recognise the fight.

Yet at one London show the organisers were reluctant to let him fight because of his pale, emaciated appearance. He quickly persuaded them and promptly won on a knock-out.

Wilde was unable to capitalise financially on his success during this prime period of his career because World War One was in progress and he was serving his time as a physical training instructor in the army. He beat one of the great featherweights, Joe Conn, in a wartime charity contest, but as the army would not allow him to fight for a money purse, his wife was presented with a bag of diamonds worth £3,000 a few days later.

There came global recognition as World flyweight champion when he battered Young Zulu Kid to defeat, also in 11 rounds. With the war now over he could embark on an American tour. His reputation was enhanced with victories over some of the best flyweight and bantamweight fighters. He returned undefeated after 12 contests.

With no fighters left at his own weight able to give him a contest, the Welshman had to resort to fighting much bigger men to make money. He reluctantly agreed to fight Pete Herman, a more than useful boxer and the World bantamweight champion.

There were a series of pre-fight wrangles. One of the ways of giving Wilde a fighting chance against bigger men was to stipulate a weight that would force his opponent to take to the Turkish bath in a bid to sweat some of his strength out of him.

Herman arrived overweight, meaning Wilde would be

conceding almost a stone. The fight was called off, but the intervention of the Prince of Wales, who was at ringside, persuaded Wilde to fight.

When he reached the ring, the prince shook the game boxer by the hand and thanked him for accepting the challenge. Wilde then asked the MC to announce that because the fight was no longer at the stipulated weight for bantams, all bets should be called off. The Welshman made a brave effort, but suffered a heavy defeat, taking a beating from which his career never recovered, although there were suggestions that even in this contest it was no longer vintage Wilde. The referee stopped the fight in the 17th round and had to carry the boxer back to his corner.

Wilde retired after that fight, only to be tempted back into the ring after two and a half years with an offer of £13,000. His opponent was to be the new star of the boxing world, Pancho Villa, at the Polo Grounds, New York. Wilde was by now 31 and was completely washed up. Villa outclassed him and he went down in the fourth but recovered and battled on. Despite his years and period of inactivity, he made a courageous defence against a fighter nine years his junior. The end came in the seventh after sustaining a terrible beating when he was knocked-out and lay face down on the canvas. Both his eyes were completely closed.

Thirty years later, he recalled: "I was so badly injured that four months passed before I was able to recognise anyone; four months curtained off from the rest of my life and of which I have no knowledge."

Wilde continued his interest in boxing and wrote for newspapers on the sport. In the 1930s he was also a leading figure in the newly formed Boxers' Union which in its short life campaigned for boxers' rights.

His fighting career should have been over, but sadly it was not. Somewhere, probably in Cardiff, lives the last man to knock-out the greatest flyweight of all time, but he would be well-advised not to broadcast the fact. Wilde was 72 at the time and he never recovered from the beating at the hands of a mugger who attacked him on a deserted railway platform. He lived out the last four years of his life in Cardiff's Whitchurch Hospital, unaware of who he was or the scale of his achievements in the ring. He died on 10 March 1969, not knowing that his wife Elizabeth, who had been so central to his success and happiness, had died almost three years earlier.

While Driscoll dominated the featherweight division and Wilde was the best flyweight, Wales's greatest period of boxing supremacy was completed at lightweight with Freddie Welsh.

Unlike most of the great boxers, Freddie Welsh was born to comfortable surroundings. His father was a very successful auctioneer in his hometown of Pontypridd. Frederick Hall Thomas was a sickly child and while very young developed signs of consumption.

His parents were advised by doctors to send him where he could get plenty of sunshine. They decided that California would be the ideal place for him to recuperate. A physical culture expert was hired to look after the boy and to build some muscle on his frail body. Boxing was not what the parents expected to be advised, but they were assured it was the finest sport to improve their son's lungs.

What surprised everybody was the aptitude the young boy had for fighting and after a while he became so accomplished that it was apparent he could make a good living at the game. Twenty years later the sickly boy from

Pontypridd would become World lightweight champion. To keep from his mother the fact that he was boxing, he adopted a ring name and the suggestion 'Welsh' came from his wife in honour of the land of his birth.

The world capital of boxing at the time was New York. This is where budding professionals could earn the highest purses. Welsh quickly established himself as one of the leading lightweights on the East Coast with a string of victories over respectable opponents.

His career was progressing smoothly until news came that his mother was dying and he sailed for home. The news of his fighting exploits arrived home before him and he was soon boxing in London at the National Sporting Club. He met with the same success on both sides of the Atlantic.

Welsh was a shrewd operator inside and outside the ring. He was a master at negotiating the best purse and supplemented his earnings with side bets. He would undertake bizarre arrangements such as taking on two highly-regarded opponents on the same night. He would receive the purse only if he stopped both men, with a side stake that both fights would end inside the distance. Even with one of the opponents being the 9st 6lbs champion of England, Arthur Ellis, Welsh still won the money.

Welsh's gift for spoiling tactics and general evasiveness and his willingness to adopt rough-house tactics when necessary did not always appeal to the crowd, but while the fans might jeer him, he still got the decisions.

In fairness, the American champions of the day were unwilling to risk their crowns against a boxer of Welsh's ability and although he continued to win fights both at home and in the United States, he was denied a World title chance.

That ended when the World champion, Willie Ritchie,

indicated he was willing to fight for a £5,000 fee whatever the result. The only impresario to be found to put up this unprecedented sum for a lightweight fight was the Englishman C.B. Cochran. The contest was staged at Olympia in London, a fortnight before the outbreak of World War One.

The Welshmen in the city acclaimed their champion with a rendition of *Land of My Fathers*. The anthem ended with cheering as the fighters entered the ring. Welsh won a points decision and considered it the best bit of business he had done in his life, despite receiving barely enough money to cover his training expenses.

He returned to America to fulfil a five-year plan. He would fight for mammoth purses and hide behind the no-decision rule to ensure he could only lose his title by a knock-out. During the war he served as a captain in the US Army, helping to rehabilitate wounded soldiers at the Walter Reed Hospital, Washington DC.

Welsh was to suffer an inside-the-distance defeat against Benny Leonard, who he had twice previously beaten. The American stopped the now 31-year-old Welshman in the ninth round. His daughter, Betty Efferson, remembers her father commenting: "Leonard was always a good fighter, but he learnt his boxing in the ring with me."

When he retired from the ring, it appeared his dream of using his earnings to fund the rest of his life would succeed. He bought a health farm. But it was just before the Depression and his money was soon gone.

A wealth of material kept by Freddie Welsh has recently come to light and been donated to the National Museum of Wales by his daughter who lives in New York City and was tracked down by a cousin in Wales who placed an advertisement in a Welsh newspaper printed in the United States.

She remembers seeing her father spar and a picture of her brother being taken with one of the boxers at a training camp, but in the main the children were kept away from Welsh's work.

"My parents didn't like us being caught up in the fuss and the media attention. I did not see my father box, but I remember Jack Dempsey coming to the house on one occasion and we knew my father didn't eat meat when he was training for a fight," she said.

The last time she saw him was when he came to the private school she attended and brought her a pair of ice skates as a present. During her childhood she was aware of her father travelling a lot for his boxing and after his retirement his devastation at a house being vandalised.

He was found dead in his New York apartment on 29 July 1927. His death is still shrouded in mystery with many claiming that poverty drove him to take his own life. Betty Efferson believes he died in his sleep, but said: "The book he was reading was left open on a passage about Eternal Life."

She added: "My overriding memory of him is of a man who was gentle. He was in a vicious type of work, but that belied the man he really was. He was a learned man who liked reading and was interested in philosophy. He enjoyed his work in physical therapy in the war, helping get people in good health."

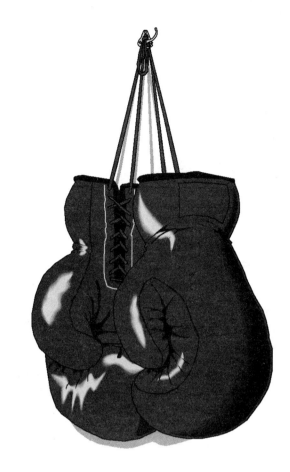

Chapter
Three

The Irish at Home and Abroad

THE Irish and their descendants continued to enjoy success in the United States, but there was also a thriving boxing scene back in Ireland for those who opted not to make the Atlantic crossing.

In the States the two men who were to dominate the heavyweight division after World War One were both of Irish stock: Jack Dempsey had Irish and Cherokee Indian blood, while Gene Tunney was second-generation Irish.

Dempsey ranks as one of the greatest heavyweights of all time. He was a box-office magnet because of his colourful style of fighting and his capacity to settle a contest with one blow. He was champion for seven years.

His real name was William Harrison Dempsey, but he took the name Jack in honour of the great middleweight champion of the last century. A former miner, his career began as a hobo fighting anyone for small stakes. He did not always win.

Yet when he won the title by beating Jess Willard in three rounds on 4 July 1919, under a blazing Toledo sky, it heralded the beginning of a golden age for boxing and the punishment which Dempsey inflicted on the champion revealed the animal-like fury that would have the crowds flocking. He won an encounter with the popular French boxer George Carpentier, the World light-heavyweight champion, for the first million dollar gate in boxing history. Dempsey won the New Jersey contest in the fourth round before more than 80,000 people.

Dempsey was now a national hero and for two years did not fight but concentrated on business interests. When he returned to the ring, the victories were amassed and the bank balance swelled. They included his stunning victory over Luis Angel Firpo, of Argentina. Firpo floored the champion twice in the opening round, including knocking Dempsey through the ropes and out of the ring.

If spectators had not pushed him back, the title would have been lost. As it was Dempsey went on to floor Firpo seven times in the first round and twice in the second before knocking him out.

While Dempsey reigned, Tunney, whose father was from Killeaden, near Kiltimagh, County Mayo, and his mother from Gortgorff in the same county, was eliminating all the other contenders one-by-one to earn the right to challenge the champion. Tunney was a natural lightweight although he never held the World crown at that division because the reigning champion, George Carpentier of France, was unwilling to travel to the States to meet him.

And it was in a lightweight contest in 1923, when he defended his American title, that Tunney received one of his worst beatings, at the hands of Harry Greb, a dirty fighter who broke Tunney's nose with a butt in the opening round and then handed out a 15-round pasting.

The only defeat Tunney suffered provided a valuable lesson and he was to retake the title from Greb only nine months later. Then, to show he had also absorbed the finer points of illegal fighting, in a return it was his turn to break Greb's nose with a butt before beating him to a pulp.

For the fight to fulfil his greatest ambition, and take the heavyweight crown from the great Jack Dempsey, Tunney taught himself to box on the retreat to counter Dempsey's aggressive style of boxing. And although he was the clear outsider to the 135,000 people who paid a record $2 million to watch the fight on 12 September 1926, Tunney produced the best performance of his life and at the end of a tense fight he took the title.

The return was an instant sell-out and as champion Tunney received $990,445, the biggest purse ever received by any boxer before the days of television. The contest, in 1928, produced the famous 'long count' of 14 seconds. Dempsey dropped his rival in the seventh round, but jeopardised his chances of regaining the title by hesitating before going to a neutral corner, thus giving Tunney the chance to recover and go on to win on points.

While such encounters were enthralling America, Irish fight fans did not have to rely only on distant bloodlines to find boxers to support. The Emerald Isle produced a few champions of its own in the first three decades of the century.

The first Irish-born World champions were the Gardner brothers, George and Jimmy, of Ballinslacken, County Clare. Their father, Pat, was a former bare-knuckle battler and he moved the family to Lowell, Massachusetts.

Younger brother Jimmy won a claim to the World welterweight title after beating Jimmy Clabby in 1908, but the division was in disarray at the time and his claim was not taken seriously.

However, his record of only six losses in 100 bouts in a career lasting 11 years was an impressive one.

George, on the other hand, took advantage of the advent of a new weight division to become only the second-ever light-heavyweight champion. A newspaper owner and boxing manager, Lou Houseman, introduced the division.

He managed a middleweight, Jack Root, who was struggling to make the weight in the division but was too light to compete with the best of the heavyweights of the time. A grade between the two won popular support and the light-heavyweight contest was born. Houseman's boxer Root duly won the first contest by defeating Kid McCoy in Detroit on 22 April 1903. Gardner believed he should have had a chance at the title and a match was made.

The Irishman's day of glory came on 4 July 1903, when he took the World title from Root in 12 rounds. His success was short-lived, however, as the new title was to change hands three times in its first year.

The legendary English fighter Bob Fitzsimmons had become known as the scourge of Irish fighters having relieved Nonpareil Jack Dempsey of his World middleweight title and defeated Peter Maher and Tom Sharkey in his career. Gardner would have been well advised to give Fitzsimmons a wide berth.

Fitzsimmons was now in his 41st year, but had not finished collecting championships in what was a remarkable career. He beat Gardner with ease and ended a reign that had lasted only four months. Gardner did fight again, with varying degrees of success, before marrying into wealth, retiring and living in comfort until his death aged 76.

While America continued to be the land of hope and glory for Irish boxers, there were healthy signs of increasing activity on the domestic front. Those fighters who chose to pursue their careers in Ireland found plenty of opportunity, at least up until the outbreak of World War One.

Many of them elected to enlist in the British forces but their active service did not preclude them from the less hazardous occupation of fighting with gloves. Boxing servicemen often bore their rank alongside their name, as in the case of Irish heavyweights Petty Officer Matt Curran and Private Dan Voyles.

At a time on the home front when heavyweight talent was limited, Curran won the Empire title in a contest with an Australian, Bill Lang.

It was a curious affair with Curran slipping on the opening bell and Lang then disqualified for hitting him when he was down. The next month Curran himself was disqualified for butting an opponent and his career never really recovered.

Among the regulars on boxing promotions in Ireland was the only black man to win an Irish championship to this day, 'Cyclone' Billy Warren. He was a black Australian whose travels took him to Dublin, where he married a local girl.

A huge man, he was a familiar character with his bowler hat, cane and faded crombie overcoat as he stood every day outside the GPO in O'Connell Street right up to his death in 1951.

In the ring his greatest achievement was taking the title from the Wexford blacksmith Jem Roche, but he lost the subsequent rematch shortly afterwards. Warren was still boxing at 50.

The highlight of this period of Irish boxing came with an historic landmark when on St Patrick's Day 1908, the World heavyweight championship was fought on Irish soil for the first and only time.

Some of the more sensitive fans would prefer that the occasion be quietly forgotten, for the contest marked another record in boxing annals. The bid of Jem Roche to take the title from the Canadian Tommy Burns lasted exactly 88 seconds and that included the time it took the referee to count him out. It remained on the list as the shortest World heavyweight title fight for 74 years.

By right Roche has no place in the ring with a World champion. He just happened to have been in the right place at the right time as Burns picked up some useful purses on a world tour.

Burns's main aim in making the trip was to avoid his most legitimate challenger, Jack Johnson, the brilliant black Texan, at least until a suitably lucrative purse could be put up for the contest. The National Sporting Club in London could not provide it and certainly there was not enough money in either France or Ireland. But in the meantime Burns was happy to take on worthy locals and Roche had his chance.

Without doubt, though, the announcement that the World title fight between Roche and Burns had been secured for the Theatre Royal in Dublin caught the public's imagination. Every one of the 3,000 tickets was sold well in advance with plenty of takers for the outrageously-priced black market seats.

When the biggest fight night in Irish boxing history was announced, Roche became a national hero overnight. Even people with little interest in boxing became instant fans. Roche's rail journey from Wexford to Dublin was like a royal procession. Cheering crowds lined the platform at every station and wherever the train stopped he got out and made a speech. As they neared the completion of their training, a national newspaper sent each man a telegram inquiring about their condition. "Just fine," replied Burns. Roche, with most of his poundage consisting of fat which hung in unsightly rolls over the top of his trunks, sent the message: "Fatter, but fitter."

Roche emerged from his dressing room to make his way to the ring to the strains of *The Boys From Wexford*. Within a minute and a half of the bell he was on the canvas.

There is a much-repeated story, now a part of boxing folklore, of how one member of the audience dashed out of the theatre as the referee finished counting and announced to the milling throng: "It's terrible in there. They're killing one another. There's blood everywhere. I can't stand any more of it. Who wants to buy my ticket?" After a mad scramble for the ticket the delighted purchaser made his way in, only to be carried out on the tide of the emerging crowd.

Incidentally, it was to be in Australia that Johnson finally caught up with the champion after a local promoter put up the largest sum ever offered to a fighter. For a guaranteed $30,000, Burns climbed into a ring in Sydney and took a battering until the police stepped in to call a halt in the 14th round.

Back in Ireland, Roche did fight again, but quickly returned to Wexford and to his first love, Gaelic football. He helped his side to an unprecedented four consecutive all-Ireland championships. Roche was 56 when he died and a plaque in the Bull Ring, Wexford, erected by his admirers, perpetuates his memory: 'A great fighter, great sportsman, but greater still in his own simplicity and modesty.'

Welsh featherweight champion Jim Driscoll had published a boxing textbook, which was to become the 'Bible' for a future World champion from Dundalk, County Louth. Tom McCormick practised the routines before a full-length mirror until he had them perfected. A string of victories took him to the verge of a British title fight, but his ambition was thwarted when champion Johnny Summers took off for a tour of Australia. Rather than hang around and wait for his return, the Irishman set off down under after him.

An Australian promoter spotted the attraction of the fight and a match was made for the title, although the National Sporting Club refused to recognise the fight. It did not matter to McCormick whose victory set him up for a fight against the Dane, Waldemar Holberg, a claimant to the World welterweight championship. The Dane was disqualified for a low blow and McCormick was declared the new World champion.

While still in Australia, McCormick put all his championships on the line against the experienced Englishman Matt Wells. He lost a clear points decision and was now champion of nowhere. His contract with the Australian promoters completed, he sailed back to England richer in pocket and experience, but minus his hard-won honours.

World War One was now in full spate and McCormick rejoined his old Manchester Regiment, with whom he had served as a boy bandsman. He could have stayed in England as a physical training instructor but volunteered instead for overseas service in 1916.

He was in Italy for the big push of that July. The Manchesters were ordered over the top and withstood a heavy shell barrage and withering fire.

Crossing a strip of land between two lines of trenches, McCormick joked with his friend and sparring partner, Cpl Jim Winspear, to be 'careful where he trod'. A shell burst between them. Winspear was maimed while Sgt Tom McCormick was killed instantly at the age of 26.

Irish boxers continued to see America as the land where boxing rings were paved with gold, but despite producing a string of ex-patriot World champions, no Irishman had won a World title on Irish soil. The first man to achieve that feat was Mike McTigue, and he did it on St Patrick's Day, 1923.

Michael Francis McTigue was born on a farm in the parish of Kilnamona, County Clare, on 26 November 1892. One of 12 brothers and a sister, he took a job with a local blacksmith to raise the fare to emigrate to the United States.

It was while working as a beef handler on New York's West Side that he proved himself to be useful with his fists. His foreman was attacked by a drunk and McTigue intervened to flatten the aggressor with a single punch. McTigue fought for 13 years in the New York area without ever coming close to getting a shot at a World title. Never considered a knock-out specialist, he was not regarded as big box office in the States and in 1922 he decided to return to Ireland.

To supplement the cost of his trip he had four fights in England en route, winning all of them inside four rounds. Irish promoter Jack Singleton was ringside at one of the fights and a delighted McTigue was told he could have a World title fight in Dublin on St Patrick's Day the following year.

Boxing historians rank Battling Siki as one of the greatest

optimists in the sport's existence. The man from Senegal decided to risk his World title against an Irishman in Dublin on St Patrick's Day and expect to keep it.

In fairness, Siki's manager must have looked at the 32-year-old McTigue as a fighter past his best with a record that, while reasonable, was not outstanding. He was perhaps blissfully unaware of the implications of fighting an Irishman in Dublin in the middle of a civil war. The promoters' main worry was getting Siki to travel by sea as the champion was terrified of water. The problem was overcome by filling Siki with wine and spirits before the journey.

Siki had come by the World crown by a curious route. He faced the legendary French fighter George Carpentier in a title fight in Paris and looked visibly frightened as he entered the ring.

Carpentier, though, was in no hurry to complete the night's work, having been persuaded to make the fight last for the film cameras that were recording the proceedings.

Thus a frightened challenger faced a champion anxious to hold him up for the first few rounds — a plan of action scuppered when Siki managed to connect with a wild punch. Dazed, Carpentier found himself on the receiving end of a battering until he was knocked-out in the sixth. Newsreels of the time captioned Siki as 'The man who beat Carpentier,' in a bid to drum up trade for a fight involving relatively unknown boxers. It needed some selling in what proved an uninspiring contest.

The opening four rounds were a cautious affair with Siki doing most of the attacking but struggling to pierce McTigue's guard. Part of the reason for McTigue's defensive approach was an injury to his thumb sustained early on.

In its later stages the fight warmed up with some lively

exchanges and both fighters trying for a knock-out. Siki lacked the technique to penetrate the good defence of the Irishman and with the sole exception of Siki himself, no one was surprised when the referee raised the hand of the Irish challenger and Mike McTigue was the new World light-heavyweight champion. Supporters crowded into the ring and mobbed the new champion, lifting him on to their shoulders.

To add to the strangeness of the circumstances, the contest took place to the echo of bombs and bullets as civil war raged in the Dublin streets around the venue, La Scala Opera House in Prince's Street.

The 'Troubles' were temporarily ignored as 1,500 spectators inside the theatre merged jubilant voices with the thousands outside awaiting news of the outcome. The announcement that McTigue had become the first Irishman to win a World title on native soil caused an explosion of cheers to rival the mine blast that rocked the city just before the fight.

While McTigue quietly enjoyed the feeling of being World champion, Siki continued on a downward slide that was to end with his bullet-riddled body being found in the gutter of the notorious Hell's Kitchen area of New York.

McTigue returned to America to enjoy the fruits of his triumph. He fought a draw with Young Stribling in front of the fighter from Georgia's southern supporters. McTigue looked to have the fight won, but the referee feared a riot if it went against the crowd's favourite and settled on a draw. It was not enough to pacify the crowd, however, and the referee and McTigue were both forced to make a rapid exit as the fans rushed the ring to get them

In a return fight with Young Stribling in the safer environs of Newark, New Jersey, the American had the better of a ten-round affair which was fought as a no-decision return contest.

Then, after a two-year reign, McTigue was relieved of his crown after a battering at the hands of the Olympic wrestling gold medalist, Paul Berlenbach.

McTigue took the loss of his precious title very badly. He had very little money to show for his years of ring toil and his efforts to find a job outside boxing, the only trade at which he was qualified, proved fruitless. In an ideal world, which boxers rarely inhabit, he would have been better advised to quit, but he fought on, losing a title contest on a points decision to Tommy Loughran. He was able, however, to gain some revenge on the former wrestler who had taken his title. Two years after Berlenbach had himself been dispossessed of the crown, McTigue confounded the pundits by hammering his way to a fourth-round victory.

Such upsets were to become increasingly rare for the ageing Irishman. Disheartened, he began to drink heavily. McTigue fought on until he was 38 years old, during which time he had been a professional boxer for 21 years. The boxing authorities withdrew his licence in 1930 after he won only one of his last six fights. After his retirement, McTigue ran a successful bar on Long Island until the late 1940s. He then succumbed to poverty and ill health. He was confined to various hospitals around New York for the last ten years of his life. Unable to recall anything of his long career in the ring, he finally gave up the fight on 12 August 1966, at the age of 74.

The tale of Ireland's other World champion during this era has a very different ending, however. No Hollywood script writer could have dreamed up as drama-packed and heart-warming a story as the true-life adventures of Jimmy McLarnin, whose boxing career, which included 13 victories over former, current or future World champions, was fashioned by Pop Foster, an English-born, battle-scarred veteran of 200 fights in fairground booths.

Foster expertly guided McLarnin to the World welterweight championship, then advised him to quit while he still had his good looks and his comfortable retirement assured. The remarkable bond remained intact right up to Foster's death at the age of 83. In his will he left his entire fortune of a quarter of a million dollars to Jimmy McLarnin.

McLarnin was born at Hillsborough, near Belfast, in 1907. He was three years old when his family emigrated to Canada to join his father's sister. One of 12 children, McLarnin did his bit to supplement the family income by selling newspapers on a street corner. Often he had to defend his pitch against covetous rivals and that was how he first learned to use his fists. He joined a boxing club and had his first meeting with the man who ran the gym and was to shape his destiny. Pop Foster, the veteran tutor, guided McLarnin through the ranks and to a fight with the current World flyweight champion, Pancho Villa, in a no-title ten-rounder. The Filipino had made his name by beating the by-then fading genius Jimmy Wilde of Wales.

The contest with McLarnin was to have a tragic aftermath. Villa entered the ring with badly infected gums following the removal of a wisdom tooth. He contracted blood poisoning and died ten days after the fight.

As an up and coming lightweight, McLarnin had a string of quick knock-outs against useful opponents but met his match in 1930 when he took on Billy Petrolle and suffered a heavy beating that might have finished the career of a lesser fighter. He was knocked to the floor in the first, but managed to go the distance despite taking a huge amount of punishment. He had his revenge with two victories over Petrolle and went on to score a remarkable series of successes.

On 29 May 1933, he got his long-awaited chance to lift the World welterweight championship. After ten years of frustration at not getting the opportunity, he took less than three minutes to knock-out the champion, the Italian Young Corbett the Third.

The Irishman rested on his laurels, enjoying the fruits of being champion for a full year less a day before accepting the challenge of Barney Ross, a Jewish fighter from Chicago who was the reigning World lightweight champion and had designs on the welterweight crown as well.

McLarnin, dubbed the 'fighter with the face of a choirboy and the heart of a killer', was the harder puncher, but Ross was the faster. In their encounter at Madison Square Garden in 1938, Ross got the decision, but such was the argument about the verdict that an immediate return was ordered. McLarnin won and regained the title.

There was an obvious need for a decider and a crowd of 26,599 paid $140,480 to witness the third fight between the two at the Polo Grounds, New York, on 28 May 28 1935, with the great Jack Dempsey as referee. Ross won a unanimous decision after an action-packed encounter that proved a marvellous advertisement for the sport.

With the World title gone, McLarnin wanted to quit right away but Foster convinced him he should go for one more big pay day. He ended up having three more big-money fights. He lost to Tony Canzoneri and then beat the man who has the distinction of holding World crowns at three weights — feather, light and junior-lightweight. He then won a ten-round contest against Lou Ambers, the World lightweight champion before retiring.

Still only 29, McLarnin took his family to live in California with more than half a million dollars saved from his ring exploits. He became a familiar face on the Hollywood scene and was a great friend of Bing Crosby. McLarnin's boxing career had taken him from the Shady Row area of Belfast to a place among the elite of Glendale, California.

The Irish journalist Patrick Myler believes the McLarnin story could not have been better scripted in Hollywood itself and his is one of the most unusual stories in the history of Celtic fighters. Foster's expertise in guiding McLarnin carefully early in his career, against opponents of lesser ability or a lighter weight, led to his protégé fighting 13 World champions during his career. All for good purses.

McLarnin was a talented boxer as Myler acknowledges: "He was a remarkable fighter, he was a good boxer and a hard puncher. He twice won the World title and retired at his peak at 29 on his manager's advice with most of his money."

The happy postscript to the story is that in 1997 and now in his 90th year, Jimmy McLarnin is very comfortable and until recently was still playing in golf tournaments with Hollywood stars. He still lives in Glendale, California.

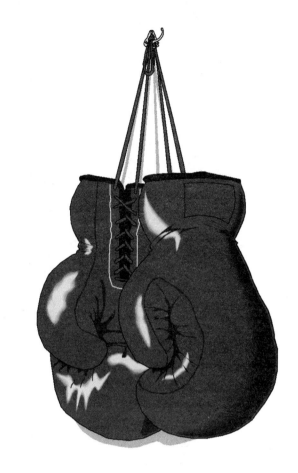

Chapter
Four

Lynch, Farr and Doyle

THE year 1913 saw the birth of three fighters who were to guarantee their place in the annals of boxing history, but for vastly different reasons.

Benny Lynch of Scotland was to prove a fighter who could beat any opponent except the bottle, and his rise as one of the great World featherweight champions was followed by his rapid demise as alcohol dissipated his talents before taking his life.

Tommy Farr from Wales was a solid fighter who enjoyed one night of glory when he carried the hopes of his nation in a heavyweight title battle against the legendary Joe Louis and, although beaten, survived the 15 rounds.

And the third of the trio was Jack Doyle of Ireland, probably the worst heavyweight title contender in British boxing history, yet a larger than life character who caught the public imagination in the Depression hit 1930s.

It was during these Depression years that the fairground booth was still the boxing school for the working classes. Tales from across the Atlantic of huge purses lured young boys to fight their way out of their surroundings. What the booths did not teach, however, was the way to cope with fame, and friends who showed the boxer the quick way to spend the purse.

Boxers have a dangerous tendency towards self-destruction. Too many of them, unable to cope with sudden fame and wealth, are swamped by their own success. So it was with Benny Lynch.

Less than a year after he was World flyweight champion he was back in the boxing booths where his career had begun, penniless and battling hopelessly against alcoholism. His is a terrible story. What seemed a climb to world fame was, in reality, a horrifying slide to death. He had a suicidal, hell-bent dive to degradation which had all the inevitability of a Greek tragedy.

Eddie Thomas, the Welsh boxer and manager, held the Lynch story up as an example of boxers generally, and the Celts in particular, to have a tendency to throw away all they have achieved.

"It is a weakness with the Celts and Benny Lynch was a prime example," said Thomas. "After all the accolades he received and all the joy his success in the ring must have brought him, he threw it all away. The bottle killed him."

Lynch came from the Gorbals, the tenement jungle of Glasgow, where he and his brother, his father and mother all slept in one bed. He was undersized and stopped growing at 5ft 3ins. The slums remained his emotional and spiritual home. He was second-generation Irish — his grandparents had crossed from Inishowen in Donegal to settle in Glasgow

— and was introduced to boxing by a local priest, Father James Fletcher, who encouraged his young parishioners to spar as a means of keeping them off the streets.

Lynch turned professional soon after his 18th birthday and joined a travelling boxing booth that toured the northern counties. He became Scottish flyweight champion at the age of 21 and had also acquired a wife, eloping to Gretna Green with Anne McGuckian, an apprentice hairdresser. Four months later they separated. Mrs Lynch had learnt at first hand what was rapidly becoming common knowledge around the pubs of Glasgow — that her husband's drinking was now a real problem.

Yet he was still able to disguise it in the ring. His early years saw him rarely fight outside his native Glasgow as he learnt his trade and established a reputation against the best of the local talent. With boxing enjoying a huge following in Glasgow, there were boxing shows most nights of the week and Lynch could move from one show to the next, picking up purses.

Since his first fight as a pro in June 1931 to his first big outing against the Italian champion Carlo Cavagnoli in March 1934, Lynch had already amassed 61 fights as well as countless rounds in the boxing booth.

In his early days he had some tough battles for purses that were less than an average weekly wage, including five against Paddy Docherty, an old friend from St John's Boys' Guild where they had boxed in their amateur days. Perhaps because the two knew each other's style of boxing so well, Docherty became something of a bogeyman to Lynch. They shared two contests each, and a fifth that might have proved a decider was drawn.

The Cavagnoli contest was a big step up for the man from

the Gorbals. The Italian had signed contracts to fight for the European flyweight title. His camp regarded the fight against the up and coming Lynch as a good test. The fight was the first staged at the Kelvin Hall in Glasgow and 10,000 fans crowded in to see the local boy take on one of Europe's finest, although the top of the bill event was a British featherweight title contest.

The main bout was disappointing and it was the performance of Lynch that gave the large crowd something to savour. Lynch won every round to lift his reputation above the countless run-of-the-mill fighters plying their trade in the city. On the strength of that success, the next major stepping stone on the path to a World title fight was to challenge for the Scottish championship title held by Jim Campbell.

Charlie Kerr was then one of a number of young boxers who used to spar with Lynch and, like him, was born and brought up in the Gorbals where fighting was a way of life.

"Like everybody else, I turned professional for the money," says Kerr, "and in those early days Benny was a great help. He would let you know if you'd done something wrong, but he didn't punish sparring partners. He was very helpful and obliging and would take time out to point out flaws."

Other Scottish boxers have gone on to win World championships and take their place in the boxing annals, but Kerr has no doubt who was the most talented.

"Benny was a wonderful boxer," he said. "He had everything. He could box, he could punch and he could think. He was so versatile. Benny was the greatest and he was a nice chap. He was taken advantage of by a lot of people and that proved his downfall."

For the Campbell fight, the sparring obviously paid off. Lynch won a points decision, but the boos that rang out from the crowd showed that not all were in agreement and there were immediate calls for a return. This time, although it again went the 15 rounds, there was less doubt about the decision and Campbell was knocked down in the last round and was tottering at the end.

Lynch was packing in a lot of fights, but many were short-lived. In his contest with Johnny Griffiths of Wales, only one punch was thrown. Lynch was ready for his World title bid.

Lynch had met the champion Jackie Brown from Manchester in a non-title fight in March 1935 that ended in a draw, although it is claimed that his manager, Sammy Wilson, had instructed Lynch to go easy so as not to scupper a title chance.

Whatever the truth of that claim it certainly hadn't deterred Brown from taking the contest and the two met again barely six months later at the Belle Vue stadium in Manchester, where Lynch became Scotland's first-ever World champion when he lifted the flyweight crown by pummelling Brown to defeat in two rounds. The champion had been on the floor ten times before it was stopped.

Moss Deyong, who refereed the contest, said that it was savage smashes to the liver that began the downfall of Brown in the fight. It is one of the ironies of boxing history that Lynch, an alcoholic, should win his World title by wreaking havoc with his fists on his opponent's liver while doing the same to his own with the bottle.

There were 20,000 people packed on to the concourse and surrounding streets of Central Station back in his native Glasgow to greet him on his return. The *Daily Record* newspaper organised a celebration dinner, where an emotional Lynch told the glitterati of Glasgow gathered there: "Thank you from the bottom of my heart. I felt I was fighting for

Scotland and my true happiness lies in the fact that I did not let Scotland down."

Charlie Kerr recalls seeing the return of the man with whom he once shared a ring and who had inspired his boxing career. "He returned to the south side of Glasgow like he was royalty. There were flags and bunting across the streets and thousands turned out to welcome him home. The Queen herself wouldn't have got a better reception."

Frank O'Donnell, secretary of the Scottish Ex-Boxers' Association, said: "From that moment Benny Lynch was a legend in Glasgow. If he sneezed there was always someone there to say 'Bless You.'"

But there were problems gathering for the new champion. He could master any man of his weight except himself. At the moment of his greatest triumph, the battle with the booze was already beginning to be lost. There would be few more glory days.

One of his supreme victories was at Glasgow in 1937 against the Englishman Peter Kane. The experts believed that the 19-year-old Kane was the best fighter in the world, but he met his match that night with Lynch. From the first round the Scot was controlling a match of epic proportions to remain the champion. It was to be the pinnacle of his career and one of the greatest fights ever seen in Scotland.

But other fights were more revealing about the way Lynch's craving for drink had closed with and outfought his passion for boxing. When he fought Len Hampston in Manchester in March of the same year as his duel with Kane, search parties had been sent out to find Lynch in Glasgow the night before the contest. He had been on a drinking binge and was dead drunk.

There were attempts to fix the fight but Hampston was

unwilling and the crowd, expecting to see one of British boxing's finest practitioners, were treated to an ugly brawl in which Lynch was put down in every round. The fight ended with a disqualification in the fifth when the men in Lynch's corner rushed into the ring to pick him up and carry him away. To make matters worse for the Glasgow man, he had split with his manager Sammy Wilson, who had guided him through the first 87 fights of his career. Once he was champion there was no end of outside advice and constant questioning of Wilson's abilities from new-found friends.

The Kane fight marked the end of the best of Benny Lynch. Within 18 months he had lost everything and was forced out of boxing by the age of 25 for constantly failing to make the weight for title defences.

His World title, for which he had trained and fought so hard to acquire through the years, was handed over at the weigh-in scales, when he failed to make the 8st limit for a title defence against Jackie Jurich. Legend has it that the night before the fight, Lynch was merely a pound overweight and his aides believed that could be sweated out without too much trouble. One night on the booze later and the champion weighed-in an incredible six-and-a-half pounds over the stipulated weight.

The American agreed to an overweight, non-title contest and Lynch gave him a pasting, knocking him out in the 12th. It was, though, a hollow consolation.

In his last fight, against Aurel Toma, it was an alcohol-soaked Lynch who entered the ring. During the fight he despairingly told his corner that he could see two opponents. He struggled to land a punch. Toma had an easy target to aim at. It was all over in the fifth.

And so was the career of Benny Lynch. He made one final

despairing effort to salvage his life by going into retreat at Mount Melleray monastery in Ireland in the hope that the peace there would help him combat the addiction that was destroying him. He only stayed a few weeks. Monks there today recall the arrival of Lynch and remember a kindly man who enjoyed a joke. He did some friendly sparring with one of the monks who was keen on boxing which proved entertaining.

Although the monastery had a good reputation for helping alcoholics, and for a time had some success with Lynch, it proved a lost cause. The boxing ability of the novice monk may have been improved, but little else was achieved in his brief stay.

As Frankie O'Donnell knows from his own experiences, locking someone away without a drink isn't a long-term solution. There has to be a change of lifestyle, which never happened in Lynch's case. He returned to Glasgow and old habits.

"Nowadays alcoholism is recognised as a disease," says O'Donnell, "but in Benny's day it wasn't. He didn't think he was drinking abnormally because he was drinking with people who also drank like that. In Glasgow at that time, people were more wary of people who did not take a drink."

He tried living in a caravan when he was promised a fight in Swansea, but one morning he was found behind a hedge clad only in his pyjamas and suffering from exposure.

The British Boxing Board of Control revoked his licence when he was found to be suffering from heart trouble. He pawned his boxing trophies to get money for whisky; as fast as Mrs Lynch got them back, he hocked them again.

Lynch went back to the booths where he had started, to take on all-comers at a pound a round. By now he was a stocky, fleshy, prematurely ageing figure, bearing little or no resemblance to the sharp-featured fighter of world fame. His home was broken, the services wouldn't take him in the war, his health was ebbing fast. His mother, who had sheltered him, died and he went to a lodging house. Finally he was so ill that the booths had no use of him either. Alone, broken and dying he was picked out of the gutter suffering from malnutrition and pneumonia. A few hours later he was dead, aged 33.

Frankie O'Donnell said: "Benny became unique, being the first to win the World title in Scotland. There wasn't the same pressure on others that followed. Being the first was a heavy mantle for anyone to carry."

The lifestyle in Glasgow was to meet your friends in the pubs and Lynch had always done that. Now, wherever he went, people wanted to buy him drinks. Lynch's problem was that he could not say no.

O'Donnell remembers that the Glasgow public would not visit the booth where Lynch was boxing. "People wouldn't abuse his memory. This was a man whose autograph they had asked for in the street and who had achieved so much for the city. The people running the booths had to take him to other cities."

The body of one of Scotland's greatest fighters lay in a vandalised grave with the gravestone taken down by Glasgow City Council. With the permission of the Lynch family, the ex-boxers raised the funds to place a headstone at the burial place.

For O'Donnell, Lynch will always have a special place in boxing folklore. "People always bring up Benny's drinking, but what I am interested in, and what people in Glasgow want to remember, is Benny Lynch the man, the Benny

John L. Sullivan, the first undisputed heavyweight champion of the world.

James J. Corbett has Cornishman Bob Fitzsimmons in trouble in the sixth round of their World heavyweight fight at Carson City, Nevada in 1897.

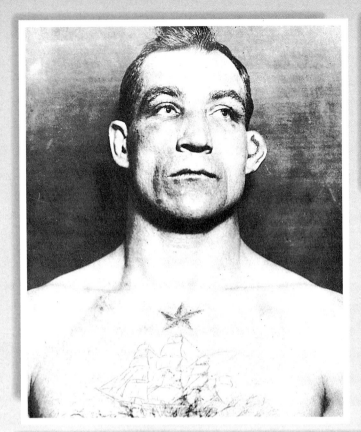

George Gardner, took advantage of the advent of a new weight division to become only the second-ever World light-heavyweight champion.

Tom Sharkey, easily recognisable with his cauliflower ear and star and ship tattoo on his chest. He fought a gruelling 25-round contest with champion Jim Jeffries for the heavyweight crown.

Jack Dempsey has Jess Willard on his knees again in Toledo during their 1919 World heavyweight championship fight.

Years later, Dempsey still looks in good trim boarding a plane at New York, en route to Columbus, Ohio, for a sports dinner.

Second-generation Irishman Gene Tunney produced the best performance of his life to take the World heavyweight title from Jack Dempsey.

Charles Ledoux's head is bowed but it was Peerless Jim Driscoll who finally succumbed in this, his last fight.

Freddie Welsh came from a well-off background. He adopted the name Welsh so his family would not know he was boxing. He is pictured here with the legendary French fighter George Carpentier.

Jimmy Wilde, lays strong claim to being, pound for pound, the best the British Isles has ever produced.

Jimmy Wilde covers up in the face of Pete Herman's onslaught. The Mighty Atom had the crowd in tears by his courageous display.

The first Irishman to win a World title on Irish soil was Mike McTigue, who did so on St Patrick's Day, 1923. Here he is pictured training for that fight against Battling Siki.

Jack Doyle, probably the worst heavyweight title contender in British boxing history, yet a larger-than-life character who caught the public imagination.

Jimmy McLarnin (left) was steered to World title glory in the 1930s by Pop Foster. Unlike many fighters, McLarnin was well-served financially by his manager.

Tommy Farr, training for his World heavyweight challenge against Joe Louis.

Farr fights back against Louis. The Welshman went the full 15 rounds on his night of glory.

Jackie Paterson telephones his wife to tell her that he has been stripped of his World, Empire and British flyweight titles for failing to weigh-in.

Benny Lynch pictured after his points victory over the American Small Montana in Glasgow, thus ending all confusion over who was the rightful World flyweight champion.

Belfast's Rinty Monaghan (right) pictured before his title defence against Terry Allen. The referee called it a draw and six months later Monaghan announced his retirement.

Lynch who brought fame and credit to Glasgow and put Scotland on the map for boxing."

Jim Reynolds, boxing correspondent of the *Glasgow Herald*, said the legend of Benny Lynch had helped in making the city a traditional boxing centre and in the eyes of many the boxing capital of Britain, whatever the claims London might make.

"Lynch is still a folk hero in Scotland." he says. "That he achieved what he did while having a drink problem makes his achievements all the more remarkable. There are still old guys about who claim to have met him. They all have stories about Benny Lynch."

—oOo—

Joe Louis, the share-cropper's son from Alabama, would dominate World heavyweight boxing for 13 years. As the champion he took on all-comers, making no fewer than 25 defences. Only three managed to stay on their feet. The first was Tommy Farr.

Farr had the stereotypical boxer's upbringing. Born to a very poor family in Tonypandy, South Wales, he worked in the local coal mine before reaching his teens. He detested the pit and the only way he could escape was boxing.

Henry Jenkins went to school with Farr and still lives in Tonypandy. He remembers Tommy and his brother, John, when they were children pushing a sack cart around the streets selling carbolic soap for the miners to bathe and vinegar from a cask as a way of supplementing the family's meagre income. Tommy was also often involved in the childhood scraps at the school that were decided on a roadway outside the school where four stones were set out to indicate a ring. Children would climb out over the school wall. One boy would bring a pail of water and a towel for the loser to clean himself up before going home.

Farr said of his decision to take up boxing: "So many people have asked me what makes a boxer. In my instance it was an escape from the strife and tribulations of poverty. I shall be ever grateful to boxing, for boxing has served me very well. I had a choice, of course. I had the coal mines or boxing and I chose what I humbly think was the lesser of two evils."

He had his first professional fight when only 12. The booth was where nearly all the great Welsh fighters before him had learnt their trade and Farr followed the trail blazed by greats such as Wilde and Driscoll. Unlike his predecessors, however, Farr's early career produced its fair share of defeats. Frustrated by his lack of progress, he walked from Tonypandy to London, but quickly realised that life was about to get much harder.

Tramping the unfriendly streets of the city looking for work was a thankless task, and trying to persuade local promoters to give him the chance to show his worth in the ring was far more difficult than Farr anticipated. All the desperate Welshman wanted to do was fight, but the London boxing scene did not want to know. Farr took any menial job he could find. He worked as a waiter and as a navvy. At one point he worked shovelling rubbish on the dockside, sleeping rough on a rat-infested barge.

When he did get the chance to fight, it proved a disaster. Randy Jones, the Welsh light-heavyweight champion, was injured shortly before he was due to fight Eddie Steel of England at the Crystal Palace. Farr was given his chance as a late replacement, but in the seventh round was caught by a punch to the throat. He immediately stopped boxing, jumped over the ropes, ran out of the arena and returned to the changing rooms. The spectators began booing, not realising that Farr had swallowed his ill-fitting gum shield, which stuck in his throat. He couldn't dislodge the shield himself as he was wearing gloves, so he left the ring unable to breath and in urgent need of assistance.

His disastrous London debut proved to be a blessing in disguise. It forced Farr to return to Wales and to a winning streak that took him to the Welsh light-heavyweight title in his home town of Tonypandy. Tommy Farr, only 19, was on his way at last.

He reacted to two unexpected defeats with an unbeaten run of victories that saw him outpoint Ben Foord to take the British heavyweight title. Farr's crouching and weaving style and accurate punches were too much for the ponderous champion to cope with and the Welshman's reputation was considerably enhanced by victories over two of the all-time greats, the German Max Baer and the Philadelphian Tommy Loughran, both former World champions.

His run of victories was to last until he stepped into the ring on 30 August 1937, to face the mighty Brown Bomber, Joe Louis, making his first defence of the heavyweight crown he had won from James J. Braddock.

At the weigh-in, Louis noticed the scars on Farr's back, a legacy of his days mining coal in narrow seams. The champion asked how he had got them and with a straight face Farr replied that he used to fight tigers at the circus for a living as a boy.

Recalling the Louis fight many years later, Farr said: "I was still a young man when I fought Louis, but by then I'd had almost 200 fights. I didn't need advice. But I always remembered what they told us in the booths when you were boxing for 15 shillings a day. If they want you to fight, you box them. If they want you to box, you fight them."

Louis had been expecting an easy affair. A nice tune-up for tougher fights that lay ahead. He was unwise to underestimate the strong Welshman who had learned his trade with countless booth rounds and fights where he would bet a half-crown on himself by putting the money on the ring apron.

The fight turned into a war. At the end of 15 brutal rounds before a 32,000 crowd in New York, Joe Louis was still the World champion. Farr had been beaten, but it was close — although not as close as the myth that grew up back home that the champion was lucky to get the verdict.

Herb Goldman, editor of *International Boxing Digest*, said: "Nobody gave Farr a ghost of a chance with Joe Louis, but he put up a display of stamina, guts and some skill lasting all the 15 rounds. He covered himself with glory in that fight."

Almost every house in Wales had a light on that night, following every blow on the wireless for the first transatlantic fight to be broadcast by the BBC. Deep in the bowels of the earth, miners were kept informed of the fight's progress with details chalked on the side of the coal trucks and sent underground at the end of each round.

In Tonypandy, at four in the morning, they stood in the street and sang *Land of my Fathers*. The rest of Britain went back to bed, but Farr had earned his place in British boxing folklore. As the first Briton for nearly 30 years to fight for the heavyweight crown, he had done the islands proud.

Legend has it that the following morning, Farr was in his hotel room still exhausted and nursing his bruises from the previous night's work. His manager, Ted Broadribb, came in and said it was time to collect the money — and then needed nimble footwork to avoid the telephone directory hurled at him as he hastily retreated.

On his night with Louis, the Welshman said afterwards: "It was a good fight, a clean fight and a very hard fight. I hope to fight him for the championship again and I think I will be the new World heavyweight champion." The return was never to be.

Farr won $60,000 for his efforts. He returned to America for four more fights and lost them all, although against some leading opponents including James J. Braddock, the former World champion, who won a points decision.

In hindsight some say he would have been better remaining in Britain and cashing in on his newly-acquired fame that spread well beyond the Welsh valleys, although nowhere was his fame greater than in his home valley. Henry Jenkins recalls: "He was a hero to a younger generation who looked up to him for the fame he had brought to the valley."

When he did return home, the British Boxing Board of Control stripped him of his British title for ignoring their request to defend his championship at an earlier date. The war intervened and he never got the chance to regain the belt again.

When he retired from the ring in 1940, Farr was a wealthy man. His five fights in New York were all for large purses. He also owned a popular pub, Tommy Farr's Corner, and a busy restaurant which he called Tommy Farr's Pantry. He had invested money in a successful bookmaking business, was reputed to have won large sums gambling on dogs and horses and was also a shrewd speculator on the Stock Exchange.

What eventually happened to his fortune is still a mystery. He faced bankruptcy and returned to the ring after a ten-year absence, at the age of 36. "They never come back," is an old saying in the fight game and it was never more true than in the case of Tommy Farr. His return did arouse some initial interest and eventually he regained the Welsh heavyweight title, but his career was to end sprawled across the ropes having been battered by Don Cockle in Nottingham. Although exhausted, he recovered to take the microphone for a last rendition of the Welsh national anthem that brought the curtain down on his boxing career.

Those who knew him have nothing but praise for Farr the man. Ken Jones, the leading boxing writer, recalls how despite his toughness in the ring, forged by fights too numerous to recall, there was another side to the man's character.

"He loved poetry and singing," remembers Jones, "and like many boxers he was a gentle person outside the ring. After his death a manuscript was discovered that was his own handwritten life story that he had never mentioned to anyone he was writing."

Tommy Farr died in Brighton, East Sussex, on 1 March 1986. His record shows he won 71 of his recorded 107 fights. But the memory that remains is of a great character and that glorious night in New York in 1937. The inscription on his memorial reads: 'I claim that man is master of himself when he can stand life's blows and scars and leave this world a better place behind him.'

—oOo—

It was the bright lights of Hollywood that attracted the most flamboyant Celt to step into a ring. It was the possibility that anything might happen when Jack Doyle climbed between the ropes that brought the crowds flocking and made him one of the biggest earners of his time.

Of his career total of 23 fights, only one went the full distance. Most of his 16 knock-out wins were scored inside the first few rounds. Just as significantly, three of his six losses were on first-round knock-outs and another was in the second.

His outside-the-ring exploits as a singer, actor, womaniser and international playboy served to add to the charisma of the man dubbed 'The Gorgeous Gael'.

But cynical fight fans had another nickname for the Irishman with the knock-out right hand, but little else in the way of ring craft or technique. To them he was the 'horizontal heavyweight', probably the worst major heavyweight Britain has produced. Doyle's success came from the way he was managed and promoted and the fact his charisma and colourful character proved a mask for his lack of boxing ability. He attracted crowds to boxing who had never been before and had a particularly large following among the women.

Nature had given him all the natural attractions anyone could ask for. A magnificently proportioned 6ft 4ins and weighing 15st, he was strikingly handsome with a fine tenor voice which enabled him to pick up ready cash when the boxing ring lost its appeal for him. He earned an estimated quarter of a million pounds in his heyday and spent it as quickly as he got it, but there was none of the trappings of easy living when Joseph Alphonsus Doyle was born one of six children of a hard-working quarryman at Queenstown, County Cork.

Already a strapping six-footer at 16, Jack lied about his

age and joined the Irish Guards, whose minimum recruiting age was 18. Entered for his battalion's boxing championships against his wishes, he proceeded to dispatch each of his three opponents in one round apiece to win the cup. He was bitten by the boxing bug.

A string of sensational wins put Doyle at the forefront of the challengers for Welshman Jack Petersen's British heavy-weight title. He was still only 19, was invited to dine in London's most fashionable restaurants and there was hardly a party of note that did not have the name Jack Doyle on the guest list.

Every one of the 70,000 seats was sold out at the open-air White City stadium for the Petersen-Doyle clash on 12 July 1933. Jack Petersen, from Cardiff, was an outstanding ama-teur and therefore attracted a syndicate of wealthy sportsmen to guide his professional career.

Although his own father had been a boxer, it was hoped the young Petersen would study to become a doctor. Jack had other ideas and took himself off to Cardiff docks where, in a pub above a gym, he was taught the art of boxing by a one-legged former sea captain. His early career did not go well. He entered the Welsh ABA tournament at three different weights and was given a hiding in all of them. His sisters had to smuggle him back into the house lest his disapproving parents saw his black eyes and bloodied features.

From these early setback, though, he prospered and although a natural light-heavyweight he fought in the far more lucrative top division. His backers formed the Stadium Club, using Holborn Station as their headquarters. Petersen was drawing huge crowds and within 18 months he was the British heavyweight champion.

The Welshman frustrated Doyle and the Irishman was

eventually disqualified in the second round for a succession of low blows. For Petersen it meant the Lonsdale Belt was his own property for his third title victory. He would fight eight British championship bouts in the 1930s, although he never got a chance at the World title.

David Petersen remembers seeing the box that his father had worn for protection in the fight and it looking like corrugated iron from the low blows Doyle had thrown.

He said: "It was disgraceful. I think Doyle was terrified. My father had a good record and carried a strong right hand and had developed a punch into the solar plexus that had many strong men writhing in agony.

"Within seconds of the fight, Doyle delivered a low blow. In the first round there were four of the most blatant low punches. That should have been it, but there were many more to come in the second."

He believes that the fight was one of those occasions where the promoters got greedy and were more interested in making a killing than a good match. In his view the contest should never have taken place.

"As far as an exhibition of the noble art of boxing went, it was an outrage," he said. "Doyle was nothing more than a bar room brawler. My father had been on a roll, but had to take a break for several months to recover from the low punches."

The British Boxing Board of Control withheld Doyle's purse after the fight and then won the ensuing court room battles to keep the £3,000 Doyle claimed he was owed.

Doyle had now lost interest in boxing. He had discovered he could pick up £200 a week singing on the stage without risking his good looks in the ring. He celebrated his 21st birthday with a party in a Dublin hotel for hundreds of guests who got through 100 gallons of champagne. Then

Hollywood beckoned and Doyle made a couple of forgettable films, married starlet Judith Allen in a Mexican registry office, and prepared to make his American ring debut.

After three quick knock-out victories, Doyle was matched against Buddy Baer, the 6ft 6ins younger brother of the former World champion Max Baer. The contest at Madison Square Garden was another one-round sensation, only this time it was the Irishman who ended up on the canvas. Doyle had blown a kiss to his wife at the ringside and turned around to see the massive figure of Baer bearing down on him. It was the end of Doyle's bid to be a World title contender.

He returned to England and found comfort in the welcoming arms of Delphine Dodge-Godde, heiress to the motor car millions. A proposed fight with Tommy Farr fell through and Doyle returned to America. And more trouble. His wife, Judith, served a law suit on Delphine Dodge-Godde for 'alienation of my husband's affections' and at the same time asked Doyle for a divorce.

Meanwhile, the heiress's father offered Doyle $50,000 plus a monthly payment of $100 for the rest of his life if he would leave his daughter alone. Doyle accepted.

Back in the United States, Doyle got into an argument at a party with a fiery Mexican actress, Movita, and ended up marrying her in a civil ceremony three days later. It was a stormy relationship from the beginning. The couple teamed up for a variety tour of the United States, Britain and Ireland. Their theme song was *South of the Border* and their duet always brought the house down wherever they appeared.

As if to cement their acceptance by the Irish, they decided to get married in a Catholic ceremony in Dublin at St Andrew's Church. It was an occasion that brought the city centre traffic to a standstill. However, their stage earnings were not enough to sustain their lifestyle and at times of financial trouble, Doyle always returned to the ring. He was knocked-out twice by Englishman Eddie Phillips inside a total of three rounds and this double disaster finished Doyle as a box office attraction in England.

The first Phillips fight ended in the sort of farce more in keeping with a Hollywood comedy. Doyle was the favourite but in the second round he rushed at his opponent, missed him completely and ended up outside the ring. He failed to get back in time to beat the count.

The Irish were more forgiving. Now 30 and overweight, Doyle had two more fights in Dublin and, despite talk of more title contests, his only subsequent ring appearances were as an all-in wrestler. Gone forever were the champagne parties, the luxury hotels and limousines. Gone, too, was Movita. She walked out on him in 1945. He did not hear from her again until ten years later, when she wrote saying she wanted a divorce to marry Marlon Brando.

Doyle replied there could be no divorce as they had married in a Catholic church. Not even a personal visit from Brando could change his mind. In his later years, life held more downs than ups for the former playboy. He divided his time mostly between the local public house near his London flat and the bookies. He would buy drinks for cronies when he had the cash and accept their charity when he hadn't.

Harry Mullan, the editor of *Boxing News*, recalls when he first arrived in London in 1964, he was in a pub in Notting Hill where an elderly figure was singing and coming round with a hat.

"Somebody said to me, 'That's Jack Doyle.' I couldn't believe it. I'd read stories about the man, and here was this shambling figure singing for a few pence. In the end, his is a very sad story," said Mullan.

However, fellow journalist Patrick Myler sees things in a different light, describing Doyle: "One of the great characters of Irish boxing. He's the great 'if only' character. He had so much potential, so much of it unfulfilled.

"But, there again, did he see it as unfulfilled. In his view he enjoyed himself. Most people say he wasted his money, but that's a matter of interpretation. He always said when he had money he spent it and when he did not his friends helped him out."

Doyle hit rock bottom in 1966, when he was fined £5 for stealing a packet of cheese from a supermarket. He still continued to earn a few pounds singing in pub cabarets or selling his story, generously embellished, to newspapers.

After his death on 13 December 1978, his body was taken home to Cobh to be buried. Over 1,000 people attended his funeral and a wreath in the shape of a boxing glove was laid on his grave by the Cork Ex-Boxers' Association.

Myler says: "People still say, if only he had looked after himself he could have been the greatest Irish boxer of all time. That's exaggerating things, I know, but there is that mystic memory of the man."

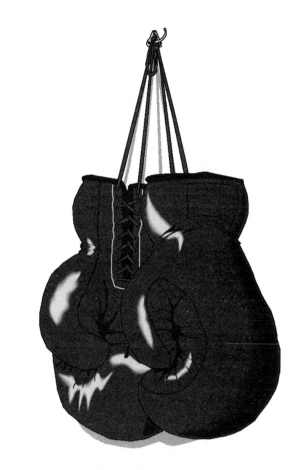

Chapter
Five

Belfast, Fighting Capital of Ireland

B OXING'S Golden Era ended as America marched off to war in 1941. Boxing was put on ice as the greatest host of fighting personnel ever marshalled were under arms, including five of the current World champions.

Joe Louis, Gus Lesnevich, Tony Zale, Freddie Cochrane and Willie Pep went to war. Their titles were frozen for the duration. When normal service was resumed, the Celts renewed their assault on World championship honours, especially in the flyweight division.

It produced one of boxing's great rivalries. Rinty Monaghan of Belfast and Jackie Paterson of Springside, Ayrshire, dominated the 8st division and followed in the great tradition established by Jimmy Wilde and Benny Lynch.

Rinty Monaghan was born in Little Corporation Street, a narrow and shabby district of Belfast, on 21 August 1920. His real name was John Joseph Monaghan but his speedy footwork earned him the nickname Rinty after the dog in the old silent movies. He began boxing in the professional ranks at the age of 14 at the city's Chapel Fields, where the crowds were hard to please and the pay was derisory. From this humble beginning he was to emerge as the first boxing superstar produced by the Celtic countries after the war.

Dennis O'Hara, boxing correspondent of the *Belfast Newsletter*, believes: "If he were around today I would imagine Rinty would be a multi-millionaire. He was a very popular man and perhaps before his time. He was the first boxer to emerge from Belfast on to the world stage."

In his home city, an unbeaten record quickly established Monaghan as a big attraction. His first set-back came when he was 17, and he crossed paths with another 17-year-old having only his second professional fight.

Jackie Paterson arrived in Belfast as a late replacement to face the home-town favourite. It was an intimidating prospect for the young Scot, but he stunned the Belfast crowd by flooring Monaghan twice and knocking him out in five rounds. It was a costly set-back for the Belfast man who hardly boxed again until the war was over. Paterson's victory gave him a short cut up the ratings and put him firmly on course for a shot at a World title.

Paterson had emigrated with his parents to Scranton,

Pennsylvania, when he was eight years old, but returned to box in Glasgow as a teenager, joining the Anderston Club at the age of 13 before coming under the guidance of Pat Collins in the pro ranks The youngster's progress was phenomenal. Within a year of his professional début he was the Scottish champion. Four months later he took the British title, defeating Manchester-based Paddy Ryan.

Ryan had gone undefeated in his previous 18 fights and had even managed a draw with World champion Jackie Jurich, the man to whom Paterson's countryman, Benny Lynch, had ceded his title when he failed to make the 8st limit for a title fight.

Yet in a full-blooded encounter in which Ryan was happy to stand and trade punches, the power of Paterson proved too much. Ryan was first cut and then when he was put down in the 13th and was struggling to see his opponent, the referee stopped the contest.

As a youngster, Paterson had worked as a butcher and this was said to have developed the muscles that made him the hardest hitter, pound for pound, of any Scottish fighter. A further six months on and it was the Empire crown he added to his trophy cabinet by defeating Kid Tanner of British Guyana.

The Scot was a heavy punching southpaw whose most devastating punch was a left hook, although there were a good few boxers who could testify that he packed a punch with either hand.

Paterson joined the RAF and married his teenage girl-friend Helen. Their first son died tragically in 1942 when he was only five weeks old, an event that mentally scarred Paterson and, in the view of many who were close to him, was a major contributory factor to his later drink-related problems.

Despite the set back in his personal life, he kept fighting. And winning. By the time he faced the Englishman Peter Kane for the World title at Hampden Park on 19 June 1943, he knew the champion's style intimately, having boxed many exhibitions with Kane during their shared time in the services.

Kane was by now becoming a veteran of title clashes with men from north of the border. He had twice lost to Benny Lynch, including an epic battle in 1937 regarded by many as the greatest British fight of all time.

This time the 35,000 crowd were treated to just 61 seconds of action as Paterson knocked-out the champion in the first round to take the World title. The victory also gave him a Lonsdale Belt outright. The Scotsman had touched heights he would never scale again.

Service commitments curtailed his training severely and as a result it became increasingly difficult for him to get down to the 8st limit to fight. Having won the championship, he then did most of his boxing at higher weights, fighting at the bantamweight or even featherweight limits. There was a view of many in the fight game that the 9st featherweight limit was the best for him.

In 1946 he put his titles on the line in a defence against a veteran of more than 150 pro fights in Joe Curran. There were 50,000 packed into Hampden Park to see Paterson win a points victory in a disappointing fight. It would be two years before he put his titles at stake again. Eventually, he was forced to make a mandatory defence and signed to defend his title against Dado Marino of Hawaii, but the fight was doomed from the outset. First Paterson obtained a postponement because of an attack of boils, then had to seek another postponement because of illness.

It was scheduled for the third time for 7 July 1947, in Glasgow, but five minutes after the deadline elapsed for Paterson to go to the scales, the crowd heard the dramatic announcement that he had collapsed and the doctor certified him as 'unfit to box'.

Opinion is divided on whether the collapse was a genuine medical problem brought on by trying to sweat down to 8st, or a diplomatic way of avoiding standing on the scales and forfeiting the World title for failing to make the weight. Whatever the truth of Paterson's medical condition, it did not prevent the champion being stripped of his title. The Scot's next battle would be in the courtroom to be reinstated.

The problems surrounding the fight had prompted the promoter to engage a substitute in the event of Paterson failing the weigh-in. The replacement was Rinty Monaghan.

Monaghan had boxed only once during wartime. He had joined the Merchant Navy and was shipwrecked. On his discharge he worked as an ambulance driver, serving throughout the worst of the Belfast bombings. The man who was a natural showman then found something far more to his taste. Along with two friends, Jim Hawthorne and Billy York, he formed a musical trio called the Three Hillbillies. They were recruited to entertain the troops for ENSA, including a concert within days of the Normandy landings. The assignments kept Monaghan busy throughout the rest of the war. He was chosen as the substitute following a victory over Paterson in an overweight match in Belfast in June 1946, in which he avenged the defeat by the Scotsman early in his career with a sixth-round knock-out.

A few days before the fight, Monaghan was assured that Paterson was comfortably on schedule and he left for a few days' holiday.

When he returned to Glasgow, he expected it to be merely as a spectator. As he was finishing a heavy lunch in a city centre restaurant that afternoon, he was tracked down by a search party with the news that Paterson had failed to show for the weigh-in.

Suddenly his services were required after all. He was ill-prepared and lost on a disqualification for persistent holding. However, the promoter, Jack Solomons, kept faith with the Irishman and a rematch between Marino and Monaghan was arranged for London in four months.

Belfast was like a ghost town on the night of 20 October 1947. Cinemas and public houses were deserted. Everyone had their radios tuned into the BBC for the live commentary from the Harringay Arena, London. Monaghan carried Irish hopes into the ring against the man from Hawaii in a fight billed as for the vacant World flyweight championship.

In the city's docks where Monaghan lived, loudspeakers were erected to carry the progress of the fight to the crowds in the street. Thousands crammed around 32 Little George's Street, the Monaghan's household. When the news came of the local hero's victory, bonfires were lit all along York Street, Corporation Street and on the Glenard Estate, where the new champion's mother lived.

After being awarded the verdict, Monaghan took the microphone and to the delight of the 13,000 spectators and the huge radio audience he gave a rendition of *When Irish Eyes Are Smiling*.

The fight was shrouded in controversy, however. Jackie Paterson obtained a court injunction restraining the British Boxing Board of Control from accepting as a title fight any contest not involving himself.

Clearly, the only sensible way to settle the issue was for the

Scotsman to meet the Irishman in the only place that mattered, in the ring. Belfast promoter Bob Gardner arranged the fight for the King's Hall on 23 March 1948.

At stake was the undisputed World flyweight championship, along with Paterson's British and Empire titles. The run-up to the fight was dominated with rumours that Paterson was again having troubles making the weight. Paterson must have known he could not lose the weight and remain strong, but if he could at least get down to 8st there would be a good pay day in it for him rather than merely relinquish the title.

The night before the fight was spent sweating in front of a roaring fire, smothered in sweaters, and doing occasional skipping exercises in a desperate bid to lose the excess poundage. At the last minute the Paterson party departed from Glasgow in a private aircraft and with only minutes to go before the weigh-in deadline, the Scotsman arrived looking pale and drawn and made the weight with 4oz to spare.

It had taken far too great a toll. Paterson lasted seven rounds before being carried back to his corner, unable to appreciate Monaghan leading the Belfast crowd with his signature tune of *When Irish Eyes Are Smiling*.

Monaghan was the undisputed champion and the first home-based Irishman to become a World title holder. All of his Irish-born predecessors were domiciled in the United States when they became champions.

Now 28, Monaghan had only five more fights after his success against Paterson. In the first of his World title defences he beat Maurice Sandeyron of France and in doing so added the European title to his collection that also included British and Empire crowns.

He then defended his title against Terry Allen at the King's

Hall. Referee Sam Russell, from London, felt neither man had done enough to deserve victory and called it a draw. Six months later Monaghan announced his retirement.

Recalling Monaghan's career, Harry Mullan, editor of *Boxing News*, said: "Rinty came through the mill in boxing starting in novice shows in Belfast. He was not a great fighter but had a huge heart and was a very resistant boxer.

"In the depressed times after the war, larger-than-life sporting figures were needed and Rinty's success had a considerable impact on the people of Belfast."

Sadly, the big purses Monaghan had earned did not ensure a life of ease. Fast cars, slow greyhounds and a too generous nature — he could never resist a hard luck story — combined to leave him, like so many gifted Celtic ring-men, having to work hard for a living. He needed money to support his wife and four children, one of whom, Colette, was crippled with polio. He worked driving taxis and lorries and turned to singing to earn a crust in time of need.

With his money from the ring, he had toured with his own big band but, although popular, Monaghan was not an astute enough businessman to make it pay as a commercial venture. In one of his last interviews Monaghan, still in sparkling form and ready to entertain with a tune on the mouth organ, recalled: "I lost all my money. In all I had made about £20,000, but it all went away through being too generous."

And in what would not be a bad epitaph for one of Belfast's most popular sons, Monaghan gave his philosophy on life thus: "When I'm in company I like to see the people happy. If they're happy then I'm happy."

When he died on 3 March 1984, at the age of 63, his loyal fans turned out in their thousands to pay their final tribute.

They lined the streets as the coffin was taken to St Patrick's Church in Donegal Street for the funeral mass.

Dennis O'Hara remembers an ebullient figure who always wanted to be at the centre of any party. It was Monaghan who sparked his own passion for boxing as it did for many others in Northern Ireland.

"He was," says O'Hara, "an outstanding personality. I was a youngster when he fought and my favourite memory is the pictures of him in the newspapers after his fights with the microphone in his gloved hand, singing, and his smiling face revealing the missing tooth.

"He would probably have preferred to be a world-class singer rather than a World champion boxer and at concerts and charity functions in the city for long after, Rinty would be there to perform."

Jackie Paterson fought on for three years after losing the title to Monaghan. He boxed in the very finest class until the end of his career in 1951. Less than two years later, the man who claimed to have earned £100,000 from boxing was in the bankruptcy court.

He told the hearing that he had gambled away £55,000, and given away another £25,000 and was now working in a pub in Largs. He was earning £7 per week in summer, but got no pay for the rest of the year, only free board and lodgings for his wife and two sons.

He had been introduced to gambling while stationed at RAF Bishop Briggs, near Glasgow. At first he could not go wrong: he devised a system which involved backing dogs which were well-bred but out of form, so that their odds were longer than their breeding justified.

He worked on the principle that, sooner or later, the breeding would show and if the dog lost the first time he backed it, he would simply increase the stake on it the next time.

Alex Morrison, a leading boxing promoter in Glasgow, recalls: "He was a compulsive gambler. He spent most of his time in the betting shops. One of my first memories of him is when I used to work in a scrapyard and there was what was then illegal gambling going on and Paterson was always there."

Morrison adds that he must have been dedicated as a boxer to reach the levels he got to and supports the view that he fought at the wrong weight. His trouble was also that he could not look after his money.

"When you saw him it was hard to believe he was a flyweight. He had tremendous shoulders and looked like he should weigh about 11 stone," said Morrison.

Soon he was betting up to £200 on a single race and, as his luck turned, so his money problems grew. He sold his Lonsdale Belt to raise enough cash to take his family to South Africa, where he found a job as a hotel manager.

The work did not last long and he was sacked for insulting the owner. By now he was drinking heavily and eventually his wife Helen divorced him after 23 years of marriage.

She gave him £1,000 for his fare back to London, but Paterson could not settle there and drank his way out of one job after another. In 1965 Helen agreed to give him one last chance and he returned to South Africa. After a long period of unemployment he found work as a lorry driver, but only a month later, on 19 November 1966, he was stabbed to death with a broken bottle during a brawl in a house in Amanzimtoti, near Durban.

Jim Reynolds, the boxing correspondent of the *Glasgow Herald,* remembers a tremendous one-punch boxer whose career was curtailed because of the war. "He is another folk hero in Scotland," he adds.

—oOo—

Unlike many of the great Celtic boxers, the early demise of Chic Calderwood was not self-inflicted. Life held no compensations for Scotland's unluckiest fighter. Born to an industrial heritage in the mining village of Craigneuk in Lanarkshire, Calderwood's sole aim was to become a farmer as soon as he had made enough money from the highly urbanised sport of boxing. Fate did not allow him to return to a rural life.

On 1 November 1960, Calderwood was officially rated the number one light-heavyweight contender in the world. He was the British and Empire champion and was next in line to fight the great American champion Archie Moore. The chance never came.

When the next World light-heavyweight title holder, Willie Pastrano, a man Calderwood had already beaten, came to defend his crown in Manchester in 1964, it was not to face the British champion Calderwood, but the well-connected Englishman, Terry Downes.

When Calderwood's chance finally came to fight for the World crown he was, in his trainer Dunky Jowett's words, 'three years too late'. This fight took place in San Juan, Puerto Rico, in 1965, against Jose Torres. Calderwood was knocked-out in two rounds.

That Calderwood displayed a total lack of judgment in associating with some pretty dubious characters outside of boxing cannot be doubted. He paid for his lack of judgment in full. He was imprisoned and stripped of all his titles.

There was not much to cheer in the life of Chick Calderwood after that, although his ultimate demise was horrific and terribly ironic. Speed had always been a Calderwood passion. Immediately after the British title win over Arthur Howard, manager Tam Gilmour had sharply vetoed Calderwood's declared aim of purchasing a sports car.

Yet he was driving a Mini and was doing zero miles per hour when he died. He drove up to a severe humpback bridge at Braidwood, Lanarkshire, where one car had to give way. Calderwood was waiting for his turn to cross when a heavy Austin Cambridge car driven by a young man charged on to the bridge. The speed was such that when it hit the crest of the hump, the car dived straight into Calderwood's Mini. The impact drove his car back into a nearby bus shelter. He was 29 years old.

—oOo—

Belfast was home to the greatest rivalry in Irish boxing. Freddie Gilroy and John Caldwell blazed a trail together as amateurs, won bronze medals in the 1956 Olympics in Melbourne and moved on to further success as professionals. Gilroy was from the Ardoyne district of Belfast, Caldwell was from Cyprus Street, just off the Falls Road. When increasing weight forced the flyweight Caldwell into the bantamweight division, Gilroy's natural weight, the prospect of the two meeting in the ring was inevitable.

A boxer with great crowd appeal because of his all-action style, Gilroy was a southpaw with a powerful punch which Irish journalist Patrick Myler believes made him the hardest hitter in Irish boxing history. After 13 fights without defeat, he had boxed his way to a British and Commonwealth bantamweight championship titles match in 1959 against the veteran Peter Keenan.

Keenan may have been ring wise but he was no match for the up and coming star and the referee stopped the contest in the 11th round after the Scot had been on the canvas four times. Gilroy then quickly added the European title by beating the Italian Piero Rollo.

This was a time when boxing enjoyed a great post-war popularity in Britain. Fight fans would turn out in their thousands to see a local champion, particularly one as popular as Gilroy. It meant he was able to fight every one of his five British title fights in front of his partisan home support without financial considerations forcing him to travel to the mainland, and especially London, although he did journey to the capital for European or World title clashes.

The leading promoter Jack Solomons is considered by many, including Belfast manager and promoter Barney Eastwood, the best there has ever been in the business. After World War Two, Solomons knew the public would want entertainment and he set out to provide it. It was Solomons who paired Gilroy with Alphonse Halimi, a French-Algerian Jew. On 15 October 1960, Gilroy lost a bitterly disputed decision for the World title that had the crowd booing and stamping their feet.

On the domestic scene he still reigned supreme. He knocked-out Billy Rafferty in 12 rounds to become the first Irishman to win a Lonsdale Belt outright. But there was growing pressure for what Myler describes as 'one of the most natural pairings in Irish boxing history'.

His former Olympic teammate Caldwell took the British flyweight title from the Scot Frankie Jones at the King's Hall with a third-round knock-out and after only four fights as a bantamweight Solomons had the idea of matching Caldwell with Gilroy's conqueror, Halimi.

Caldwell recalls being asked if he would take the fight at the heavier weight. "I didn't say no. I would have boxed anybody at whatever weight I was told, if it meant a chance for the World championship."

The fact there was a national revenge factor would help sell the fight and Solomon's judgment, as usual, proved impeccable. Caldwell boxed superbly. His philosophy before fights was to always respect an opponent before he got into the ring, but not once inside. In the 15th round he had Halimi down and moved in to finish it, only for the referee to give an eight count and enough of a breathing space to ensure his opponent survived the contest. Caldwell, though, had done enough to become World champion, winning a close contest on points. In a return with Halimi he repeated the victory.

On his return to Belfast, bonfires were lit and crowds gathered in the Falls Road. On the gables of the houses was written: 'Welcome home Johnnie, our champ.'

Caldwell was taken to his mother's house where well-wishers crowded in asking for autographs and photographs of the World champion. It was hours before he could get to his own home and see his wife and children.

In a fight for the undisputed World crown, Caldwell travelled to Sao Paulo, Brazil, to face the legendary Brazilian, Eder Jofre, who was too strong and hard-hitting for the Irishman, whose corner threw in the towel in the tenth round. It had, though, been an outstanding display of courage in a harsh arena.

These were the fights that should have provided long-term financial security, but Caldwell received just £1,200 for three World title fights and today is bitter at the treatment from his handlers and particular his Glasgow-based manager Sammy Docherty. The wrangle was to lead to a court case against Docherty which the boxer lost. He believes at the time he boxed there was not enough protection for fighters from the people who held the power in the game. Too many were exploited.

He said: "In those days you just took what money they said. They told you this is the money you are getting. Those in control could get away with a lot. I have nothing against boxing and boxers, but I ended up in a contract I could not break free from."

With his World title aspirations now gone, Caldwell lowered his sights to domestic level. Solomons was again involved and the scene was now set for the showdown between Gilroy and Caldwell, with Gilroy's British and Empire titles at stake.

Dennis O'Hara described it as the fight nobody thought would happen, but it did. "It was an amazing fight. It was one of the biggest nights in Belfast boxing. A phenomenal event."

Harry Mullan, editor of *Boxing News*, recalls the epic fight between the two boxers who had once shared a room as members of the Irish Olympic boxing team and believes that when friends fight it is often more intense and ferocious than a contest between enemies.

The evening of the encounter saw the young Mullan listening to the fight on the radio and putting aside his study of an epic poem in Irish that was to prove strangely apposite. The line he remembers translates as: 'It is a terrible shame to put two sons of the Gael against each other to see who is superior.'

The brutally of their trade was summed up by Caldwell

when he said: "Before a fight I go into a church and pray. I pray for myself and I pray that my opponent will not be seriously injured. Then I go into the ring and try to hurt him as much as I can."

Before a packed King's Hall crowd in their native city, the two took part in a savage ten-round fight in which both boxers were sprayed with blood, most of it coming from Caldwell's eyebrows.

O'Hara recalls the contrasting styles of the two made it a marvellous spectacle. Although both were strong punchers, Caldwell was a classical boxer who was very fast while Gilroy did not bother dancing around the ring but just went after opponents.

It rightly deserved its tag as the 'Irish fight of the decade'. Caldwell was put down in the first round but battled back and both vied for the upper hand in a contest of fluctuating fortunes. The cut that Caldwell suffered in the sixth round got worse. The fight had to be stopped. It was, believes O'Hara, a sad way for such a contest to end and the manner of it meant the finish was to some extent inconclusive. Inevitably, there were calls for a return fight, but it was not to be.

Gilroy, the winner, never fought again. There was a dispute with the British Board of Control over contracts and a fine which he never paid, thereby having his licence with-drawn. He was also having weight problems and perhaps the will had been sapped in that last epic contest.

More than 30 years on, he remembers the promoter Jack Solomons at the time desperately trying to persuade him to return, but he was adamant he was not going to and the more insistent the BBBC got, the more determined he was to resist.

However, what is not so widely known is that he did go back into training with a view to making a comeback as a featherweight, but the £2,000 fine he had hanging over him for not agreeing to a return with Caldwell tipped the balance.

"At times I am sorry that I retired so soon," he admits, "but in the long run it was probably for the best." And he jokingly adds: "Going when I did I kept my good looks and my wits about me and as my family said at the time, I may have got hurt if I'd tried to come back."

Instead he bought the Tivoli bar in Donaghadee, County Down, with all the money he had earned from boxing. At first things were going well. His boxing fame helped keep the customers coming in and pictures of him in his fight days and the Lonsdale Belt he won were on display.

The resumption of the Troubles in 1969 marked the beginning of the end for the business. "I ceased to be a sportsman and became a Roman Catholic in local peoples eyes." The pub was bombed and anti-Catholic slogans were daubed on the walls. There were threatening phone calls.

What hurt Gilroy most, though, was that the campaign was driven by people living locally. A man whose prowess in the ring had done so much for Belfast and Northern Ireland was hounded out of his business and had to take a big financial loss. Disillusioned, he quit Northern Ireland for Australia where he managed a club. He returned after his marriage broke up and turned to alcohol. It was during a drinking binge that the Lonsdale Belt, for which he had worked so hard, went missing. He knows the identity of the man who asked to borrow it while Gilroy was drunk and later claimed he gave it back and the former boxer must have lost it on a bus.

The incident happened in 1985 and the belt has not been

seen since, although Gilroy is confident that the person who has it will make a mistake and it will be returned to him. The loss of such a valued prize has had a sobering effect. He has not had a drink since and has no intention of starting again.

After their encounter, Caldwell fought on but never returned to the heights achieved early in his career. He regained the British and Commonwealth bantamweight titles he had lost to Gilroy by beating George Bowes in seven rounds. A year later the titles were again lost when he was stopped by Welshman Alan Rudkin in ten rounds. He retired in 1965.

Sadly, little remained of the substantial purses he won during his career and he found work in his old trade as a plumber before doing a variety of jobs including working in the shipyards. He worked for a while driving a taxi around Belfast. After an unrewarding spell in Canada, he returned to join the lengthy dole queues in his home city. At the age of 59 he knows he is now at the age where he will never work again.

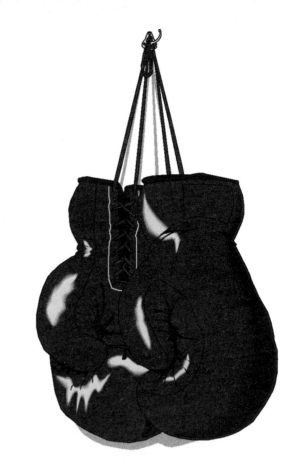

Chapter Six

The Sixties and the Rise of Winstone and McGowan

IT was nearly 40 years since Wales had a World champion, but the promoter Jack Solomons, whose domination of the big fights in post-war Britain continued, believed that was about to be put right. While on a tour of the United States, Solomons had seen the World lightweight champion Ike Williams and had not been impressed. He was convinced that the leading British lightweight champion of the time, Ronnie James from Swansea, could beat him.

And James was proven box office material. His fight for the lightweight championship of Great Britain against Eric Boon had attracted 35,000 spectators to Cardiff Arms Park. The home supporters saw their fighter knock-out the veteran Boon in ten rounds.

Williams was lured to Wales to defend his title for 25 per cent of the gate and three return air tickets for himself, his manager and trainer. James settled for 15 per cent of the gate.

The attendance at Ninian Park, Cardiff, was estimated at around 40,000 to watch the Swansea man battered to defeat in nine rounds. Solomon's judgment had been wide of the mark with James, but the arrival of a World champion from Wales would not be long in coming. The old breeding ground in the industrial valleys was about to produce one of the most famous double acts in the history of the sport: Eddie Thomas and Howard Winstone.

Eddie Thomas was born in Merthyr Tydfil on 27 July 1926. He was almost the stereotypical Welshman: a good footballer, he sang in the church choir and worked with his father and brothers in the family coal mine. His outstanding talent, though, was as a boxer. Despite his father's objections on the grounds that it was too dangerous a pastime, he learnt to fight at the Merthyr Boxing Club and developed a fast left jab that would be mirrored by the two most successful of the fighters he managed, in Howard Winstone and Ken Buchanan. He crowned a glittering amateur career with the ABA lightweight championship in 1946 and was a member of a British team that defeated the mighty Americans before he signed professional forms with manager Sam Burns.

On his début he was due to face Mickey Duff, who would make a bigger impact as a promoter than he ever did in the ring. Duff pulled out of the contest and Thomas continued on a successful path. Within three years he beat Henry Hall at the Harringay Arena to become welterweight champion of Great Britain. After the referee had raised his hand, Thomas took over and gave an impromptu rendition of *Bless This House*.

"After 15 rounds, to start singing I must have been mad," remembered Thomas, "but like all Welshmen I thought I was Mario Lanza and gave it a go. I was never allowed to forget it and wherever I went for years after I was asked to sing that song." The night of his return to Merthyr is one he would never forget.

On 27 January 1951, he fought Pat Patrick for the vacant Empire title. Thomas knocked-out the South African on a drenched canvas in the 13th round and went on to win the European title by beating Italian Michele Palermo after two knock-downs over 15 rounds in Carmarthen, West Wales.

As British, Empire and European champion, the next logical step for Thomas was a shot at the World title held by the great Sugar Ray Robinson. Boxing politics intervened and to the day he died, Thomas's great regret was that he never got the chance to compete for boxing's highest prize. He eventually lost his domestic titles and was denied the Lonsdale Belt outright after being on the wrong end of a points decision to Wally Thom, a man with whom Thomas would again cross swords in later years when Thom was a referee.

Thomas never fought for a title again, but went on to manage a world-class stable of boxers. He ran the Dowlais Boxing Club while working eight hours a day at the face in his local drift mine. At the Aberfan disaster in 1966, when a slag heap engulfed a school, Thomas was among the first at the scene using his mining experience in the search for survivors and carrying out many of the children's bodies himself.

It was in his gym, a room above the local snooker hall, that one of British boxing's most famous partnerships was forged. This is where Thomas met Howard Winstone. In his younger days when Thomas first met him as an amateur, Winstone was a bit of a slugger. The veteran told him he had to learn to box. He was a natural pupil.

Winstone was born in humble surroundings in Merthyr Tydfil on 15 April 1939. Over half a century later he still lives in a two-up-two-down in the Dowlais area of the town. In the intervening years he was one of the most famous boxers in the world.

Ken Jones, the boxing writer and journalist, pays Winstone the highest compliment. "Technically, Winstone was the best boxer produced in this country. He was supremely gifted with good balance and good feet, but he liked to fight and it did not take much to get him into a scrap."

Prior to an accident at the toy factory where he worked, that clipped off the tops of the fingers in his right hand, Winstone had gained the reputation of being a fearsome puncher. At first he believed his boxing career was over. He said: "When they took the bandages off and all I could see were these little stumps, I thought that was it. As it was I was out of the game for two years."

However, with this handicap he had to revise his strategy.

This was to be a key role for Eddie Thomas, who was a great advocate of the old ring saying that a good boxer always lasts longer than a good hitter because he takes less punishment in the long term. That includes the hours of sparring in preparation for a fight. Thomas's main objective at this point was to capitalise on Winstone's strengths of incredible hand speed and inexhaustible stamina. These boxing skills were sharpened to such an extent that the big hitters rarely laid a glove on him. He was a natural talent.

Commenting on the hand injury, Thomas said: "The accident would have broken the heart of any youngster, particularly a young fighter. But they did not reckon on the make up of this kid, with his mixture of Welsh, Irish and Jewish blood running in his veins. A richness of the finest fighting breeds in the world."

Under Thomas's guidance, Winstone won 83 of 86 fights as an amateur, culminating in an Empire Games gold medal in 1958, won in Cardiff. After the Games, and with a young wife and family to feed, Winstone decided to join the pro ranks.

Thomas put a good deal of thought into the matchmaking in the early stages of Winstone's career, mixing it cleverly with journeymen and fighters who could test his undoubted potential.

After 24 fights in just over two years, Winstone was matched with the golden boy of English boxing, Terry Spinks, for the British featherweight title. Spinks, a gold medalist at the Melbourne Olympics, was the heavy pre-fight favourite, but from the first bell Winstone was the master. Spinks, who needed only one more victory to make the Lonsdale Belt his own, had reeled into his corner at the end of the tenth round and told his cornermen he had had enough.

Merthyr gave Winstone a tumultuous reception as he rode in triumph up a crowded High Street. Flags and bunting fluttered from shops, cinemas and cafes. Thousands of fans lined the route, 20 deep in places. Some had waited two hours before the champion's open field car with a police escort nosed its way to the steps of the flag-bedecked Town Hall. As the Mayor of Merthyr, Alderman C.E. Webb, stepped forward to grasp the boxer warmly by the hand, the crowd broke through the police cordon and surged around the foot of the Town Hall steps.

As he made his way into the building amidst all the back-slaps and hair ruffling, Winstone was greeted by his two young sons Wayne, aged four, and Roy, aged three, wearing miniature scarlet boxing gloves, which were a championship present their father had bought in London. Thunderous cheers greeted Winstone's appearance on the Town Hall balcony where he waved to the vast crowd. The Mayor, a former miner and ardent boxing fan, said: "This is a red letter day for Merthyr."

Winstone was content with a few modest words of thanks to his manager and those who travelled to Wembley to cheer him. Then the cheer went up: "We want Eddie." Winstone's manager was unwillingly pushed to the front. "That wonderful Welsh singing put some hwyl into Howard," he told the crowd, "although I don't think he needed it."

The last time Merthyr had laid on a similar reception for a boxer was in 1949 when Thomas himself had brought home the welterweight championship.

Winstone's only great regret about his triumphant battle for the title and his return to the town was that his father, Howard Senior, had passed away a few weeks previously and never saw his son crowned British champion.

"He sowed the seeds of everything I achieved in boxing by buying my first pair of boxing gloves and giving me every encouragement in the early days," said Winstone.

His career was progressing rapidly with talk of European, Empire and even World title fights in the pipeline for 1963. Having reigned supreme over British challengers, it was now time to continue building his reputation on a world stage.

However, on 5 November 1962, Winstone suffered his first set-back, a defeat at the hands of the American Leroy Jeffrey. Thomas was told that the American was struggling to get fights and would be a good match for Winstone. Jeffrey's ability had been seriously undersold by the promoter. The Welshman was knocked down three times. Back in the dressing room after the fight, Winstone and his entourage were met by probably the greatest middleweight champion of all time, Sugar Ray Robinson, who was fighting an exhibition on the same bill.

Robinson took the young Welsh fighter back to the day when he lost his first professional contest and how he came to terms with the disappointment, shrugged it off and went on to become a boxing legend. When Winstone is asked today about the contest he simply replies: "Is that the one where I forgot to duck?" Those close to him believe he had got too cocky and over confident and the defeat helped concentrate his mind.

He says: "When the ref stopped it I thought I could go on but Eddie was glad. Thirty-five fights is a lot to go unbeaten and I might have been taking chances. I think the defeat taught me a lesson and I learned from it."

Thomas believed that if the fight had not been stopped it could have finished Winstone as a boxer. "I held him by the ankle and told the ref to stop the contest. You can take too much as a fighter and if he had carried on, I don't think we would have heard much more of Winstone as a boxer. As it was, with his fighting heart it wasn't hard to bring him back."

Winstone returned to the ring and was brought back with a few nice wins against carefully matched opponents. He duly took the European title from the Italian Alberto Serti in front of 10,000 supporters in Cardiff.

At this stage Winstone was rarely out of training and yet he never complained of staleness. It was a testament to Eddie Thomas's varied training regime.

This consisted of log chopping, arduous Brecon Beacon runs allied to the nightly gym sessions, where he had a variety of sparring partners ranging from bantamweights for speed and elusiveness, to heavyweights for strength and durability.

There was talk about a match for the World title with Sugar Ramos and there is some criticism of Thomas for not taking the fight. The manager had his own forthright view.

"I should have been locked up if I had taken that fight and rightly so. Ramos could take a man's head off with a punch. Solomons had printed cards saying Sugar Ramos and Howard Winstone for the title, but I did not take it and I was right I think."

With that Ramos fought Vincente Saldivar and lost his title. Saldivar would soon figure in Winstone's plans and the stage was now set for the long-awaited show-down between the two best featherweights in the world. Saldivar arrived in London with an impressive record of 26 pro fights with 25 wins, of which 21 were inside the distance. The Winstone camp knew little about Saldivar, other than he had a reputation as a brawler and, worse still, he was a southpaw, a fighter whose stance is right foot forward and who leads with his right.

There was to be no night of celebration for the 12,000 Welshmen who had made the journey to Earls Court Arena.

Saldivar's natural strength gave him the edge in a close points decision, a verdict that Thomas was none too happy about. "How he lost that decision I'll never know, nor will 98 per cent of the people who were there on that hot June night of 1967.

"I wish the BBC would show a film of that fight in slow motion so that people who only see boxing on television could see where the punches were landing. Punches which looked good on the screen were missing by six inches."

And Thomas added: "Anywhere else in the world that would not have happened and the home fighter would have got it if he was still on his feet at the end of 15 rounds, but we weren't looking for favours."

When Winstone returned to the ring he began to have problems making the 9st limit. One of Thomas's lesser-known methods of losing those vital few pounds was to make a boxer sleep on the floor the night before the weigh-in. In this he was years ahead of sports science, as sleeping on the floor with a minimum of clothing made the boxer involuntarily shiver, this is turn set off a chain reaction where to recover body heat the body burns surplus fat and thereby produces the required weight loss. Winstone himself, though, is sceptical about the success of the technique and believes the battle to keep his weight down owed more to secret trips to a Turkish baths in Newport, which Thomas never knew about.

Following a few comeback fights, including regaining the Welsh title he had held six years earlier with a win over Lenny 'The Lion' Williams of Tonyrefail, Winstone was ready for another assault on the World title, although Thomas himself was reluctant to take a second Saldivar fight, believing Winstone should consider retiring.

The second Winstone-Saldivar fight was to be one of the most controversial in championship boxing history. Referee Wally Thom, the man who as a boxer had denied Thomas his Lonsdale Belt outright, awarded the fight to Saldivar. Thomas never forgave him for that. "Howard won the first ten rounds so how could he possibly lose." It was a view echoed by the majority at ringside who thought Winstone had done enough to get the decision.

Winstone could not believe he had worked so hard and done so much and yet the title had eluded him. Saldivar had put him down in the 14th as he tired, but the early rounds had all been his. Like most of the crowd he thought he had done enough.

However, although disappointed with the verdict after he had come so close, losing by just one round, Winstone never blamed Thom or believed his defeat somehow had more to do with an old grudge with his manager than what happened in the ring.

Winstone says: "I can't say I agree with him, but I still think he acted honestly." However, it did show the wisdom in having judges doing the scoring and letting the referee get on with his job in the ring, which is now standard practice in World title fights.

Another disappointment was the size of the crowd. Thomas had taken a percentage of the gate, hoping the fight would sell but was dissatisfied with the receipts. He even sent a team of accountants to check promoter Harry Levene's figures. Two tea chests of unsold tickets told their own story.

There was by now some criticism of Thomas's management. The argument was that Winstone should have been matched with the former champion Sugar Ramos, who was just the shell of the fighter he once was before a younger Saldivar had the chance to dethrone the champion.

Years later Winstone himself still has nothing but praise for the man who guided him through his career. "Eddie was marvellous. He was a good trainer. You'd think he was my father, the way he used to keep telling me what to do and what not to do."

Thomas did secure a third fight with Saldivar, this time in the Mexican's backyard in Mexico City. Winstone, Thomas and his sparring partner Billy Thomas set off for Mexico three weeks before the fight. Preparations did not go well. Rumours were rife that Winstone's wife, Benita, was having an affair with a local man. In a close knit community Merthyr, like most valley towns, had its own grapevine system and it wasn't long before the story came to Winstone's ears. As the marriage was breaking up, a row had broken out between the couple in which Winstone was stabbed by his wife in the arm.

Thomas put it about that the injury was caused by an accident in the garden. The day before the fight his wife and her mother arrived in Mexico. Unfortunately it was to have a detrimental effect as Winstone and Benita had a furious row in his hotel.

Against the odds and a general feeling that he had already given his all in the first two title fights, Winstone controlled the first part of the contest, but by the 12th round Thomas threw the towel in, the first time he had to do it in Winstone's 60 plus fights. The boxer, in control of all his senses, was furious at the time, but relented later in the dressing room when he realised Thomas had made the correct decision.

After their three tough fights, the two boxers became good friends with Winstone paying a visit to Mexico City to see his old adversary during the Olympic Games in the city in 1968. Saldivar died of a heart attack in 1985.

Winstone returned to the United Kingdom to read a story sold to the *News of the World* by his wife. After talks with his family and Thomas, he decided to fight on. With Saldivar having announced his retirement, the next logical opponent was the Japanese fighter Mitsunori Seki, who also had three title challenges under his belt. Thomas did not want a fight with an up-and-coming challenger, but felt Seki was the right option and had been through some hard battles. He decided to move his fighter to Carmarthen to prepare for the contest. They set up camp in the local rugby club gymnasium and one of the sparring partners brought to the West Wales town was Ken Buchanan, later to gain World title honours himself.

The championship contest was to be the first World title fight to be held at the Royal Albert Hall and after nine rounds, Winstone was at last champion of the world when Seki was stopped with a cut eye. It is claimed Thomas's decision to throw the sponge into the air and climb into the ring gave the referee little option but to stop it. The boxer's stablemate, Eddie Avoth, tried in vain to clear the ring so that the formal announcements and presentation could take place and eventually after ten minutes of frantic activity, Saldivar stepped into the ring to present him with the belt.

As Merthyr prepared a hero's welcome, Winstone was granted a decree nisi on the grounds of adultery. Sir Owen Temple Morris QC, after granting the divorce, called Winstone to the bench and said: "The whole of Wales are proud of your achievements and the honour and prestige you have brought to your home town."

Thousands had been waiting all day to welcome him

home. Every available policeman was on duty. Young boys climbed lamp posts and hung from windows to get a glimpse of him. More than 6,000 were packed into the small town square. The Dowlais choir sang.

And when Winstone eventually arrived, he had to be ushered through a back door into the hall where the Mayor, Alderman Mrs Alice Evans, along with 100 special guests welcomed him to a civic reception.

After one more non-title fight, Winstone was to fight for the last time in the Welsh seaside town of Porthcawl, which was a Mecca for the Welsh mining families of South Wales in the 1960s and it was anticipated that many would attend as it was during their annual two weeks' holiday. The pre-fight preparations in Camarthen were as before and the opponent, the Cuban José Legra, was a fighter Winstone had already beaten. The Welshman's career ended in five rounds. His speed of reaction had gone.

"I was ready to get out of the game then. I had just got divorced. I was starting putting weight on. I wanted to go out a winner, but he hit me with his head," said Winstone.

He had notched up 67 fights and won all the titles. With a career that started at ten years of age he felt it easy enough to quit. There was some living to catch up on.

Thomas told Winstone to retire. He paid his protégé this tribute: "It has been my great pleasure to have had the honour of managing and training the greatest exponent of boxing that this country has ever seen and I say that with due respect to Jimmy Wilde, Freddy Welsh and Jim Driscoll — the greatest trio to have come out of Britain before Winstone entered the ring."

After his retirement there was the usual story of failed business ventures and the discovery of the dubious joys of alcohol after years of abstinence during his fighting days.

Thomas said: "Like many boxers before him, Winstone was badly advised and led up the garden path by those claiming to be his friends."

The shops and pub that should have been good money earners somehow never paid. The pub should have been lucrative but failed. He was given the licence to run one-arm bandits that were guaranteed to make 11s 6d profit in the pound, but still managed to lose on them.

Thomas explained: "It's to do with the hangers-on and backslappers; you take more punishment off the backslappers than you ever do in the ring. They want to cash in on your publicity or your public image and they all want to be in on your act.

"And they start leading you astray. It's just to show themselves off not you. You think they're your friends, but they're your biggest enemies."

After the Spinks fight, Winstone had treated himself to a holiday in Majorca and it was to remain a favourite destination. But now there were at least half a dozen people going with him and he was paying for them all.

About his drinking Winstone, at 57, says: "I was 29 when I retired and I had been training since I started boxing and was married young. I decided to enjoy myself a bit and started going out drinking with the boys. I got into the habit of drinking when I shouldn't have been."

He never thinks he had an over-generous nature, but was happy to buy a few pints for the boys in the pub. "That's what money is for, to spend." Health warnings have now curbed his drinking. With his wife he plans to carry on as he is, living in the town he grew up in.

At the same time that Thomas and Winstone were chasing the World title, another great Celtic partnership was being forged north of the border in Burnbank, Lanarkshire. In Scotland there is a great tradition of father and son fistic relationships. None achieved more than Joe Gans and Walter McGowan.

Thomas McGowan took on the name Joe Gans from one of the greats among the early lightweights. Indeed, Walter remembers he was 12 years old before he discovered it was not his father's real name when somebody in the street called him 'Tommy'.

Joe Gans, the Burnbank version, had fought on the booths under a pseudonym as was the fashion. With ten children to feed it was the only way he knew of earning extra money. At one stage he notched up 29 fights in three weeks.

He had decided that Walter, the bairn of the family, would be his heir apparent within the ropes. The youngster was used to coming off second-best in childhood squabbles and in soccer matches.

At the age of nine he was, in his words, 'dragged off to the boxing gym'. His brothers were already being coached by their father and enjoying the sport. Walter was more reluctant.

He preferred wrestling to boxing as a recreation. And the major career ambition for the man who would be a World champion boxer was as a professional jockey. Joe Gans had served in the army and got friendly with Harry Carr, who went on to become the Queen's jockey.

"My name was put forward to see if I could be coached to be a jockey," he recalls. He was also helping deliver milk and part of his task was to help out at the stables. He was allowed to ride the horses which he loved, although he was still keeping up with the boxing. It was a brief taste of the fame that goes with success that persuaded McGowan to concentrate full-time on boxing. At the age of 14 he won the Scottish youth championships and his photograph appeared in the local newspaper. That was the clincher for the young-ster. Everything else was now given up.

McGowan had a glorious amateur career that saw him lose only two of 124 fights and collect the Amateur Boxing Association championship in 1961. He also represented Scotland ten times, winning all the contests. Such was his prowess and aggression it became increasingly difficult to find opponents in the amateur ranks and at the age of 18, he turned professional.

His first fight in the paid ranks was against an ageing boxer, who in his day had been Scottish champion, George McDade. McGowan had been pestering his father to discover who his fight would be against. When he was told, he would rather have not known. "He told me two days before the fight and I didn't sleep at all. I thought I was going to get murdered."

He managed to beat his hero McDade, but is full of praise for a great character and a man who was a credit to Scottish boxing. In the end, the clock had just run out for the former champion and it was time to make way for the rising star. In his tenth fight he came up against Jackie Brown for the British and Commonwealth flyweight titles, knocking him out in the 12th. Traditionally a boxer must win three times to make the Lonsdale Belt his own. But if there are no obvious championship contenders, it is awarded after three years. This rare honour was achieved by McGowan.

An attempt to win the European title saw him travel to Rome in April 1964, where he faced Salvatore Burruni. McGowan was warned he would need to win convincingly if he was to get a decision in the Italian's own backyard. "If you want to win a points decision over there you have to knock them out," he was told.

It forced the Scot to be too aggressive and mix it too much with an experienced champion who had held the title for three years. McGowan thought he had done enough and many neutrals agreed, but after 15 rounds it was the hand of the Italian that was raised.

McGowan recalls: "I was trying to knock him out and applied a lot of pressure, but he was like a human tank and absorbed everything I threw at him. A lamp post couldn't have taken what I threw at him."

The following year he tried to win the European bantamweight title from Tommaso Galli, again in Rome, but managed only a draw, although again the general view was that he had done enough to win.

Although illustrious London boxing promoter Jack Solomons was entering the twilight of his fabulous career as Britain's foremost World title impresario, he still retained sufficient clout and cash in 1966 to command international respect.

Solomons won the right to stage the World title bout between the holder, Salvatore Burruni of Italy, and McGowan at the Empire Pool, Wembley. He was to rue the decision not to stage the fight in Scotland. A meagre attendance led to a £14,000 loss for Solomons. But those who did attend witnessed one of the great title fights.

Fighting away from Italy, McGowan could change tactics. Here he relied on his boxing skills and the Italian had to come looking for him. As Burruni came in looking to land big hooks, McGowan was able to score easily with straight lefts and rights.

The Scot was comfortably winning the fight until a clash of heads in the ninth opened a deep cut over the left eye. Three times the referee, Harry Gibbs, halted the action to look at the damage while assuring Gans to do all he could because McGowan was well ahead.

As the fight progressed, the cut got worse. McGowan remembers that there was so much blood on the floor that both fighters were beginning to slip in the ring. The Scot's cause was helped because Burruni was tiring. Before the start of the last round the veteran ref Gibbs came over to the McGowan corner and whispered to Gans: "All he has to do is stand on his feet this round and he's won it." A cut would not deny McGowan on this occasion. Scotland had a new World champion.

Joe Gans and Walter McGowan wept openly in each other's arms. They had confounded the critics and knockers and vindicated the much criticised methods of Gans.

Looking back, McGowan recalls it was a tough fight and one where he was forced to think all the way through against a strong, formidable opponent who was always pressuring him. After the fight Burrini came over and congratulated McGowan. "You were too fast, my friend, too fast." The two are still good friends.

The skin above McGowan's eye was now splitting with ominous regularity. Each fight ended in a blood bath. Cuts inevitably cost him his title against Chartchai Chionoi in Bangkok, even though he was outclassing his opponent and well ahead on points when the referee stopped the fight in the ninth.

In a return bout nine months later in London, the Scot was again stopped with a damaged eye. As in the previous contest he was in front when the fight was stopped and criticism of

Joe Gans surfaced again with the view expressed that an expert cuts man should have been in the corner to try to staunch the expected flow of blood. Gans, though, had been with his son throughout his career and dealt with the cuts in the past. It is unlikely much more could have been done.

The problem for McGowan was the cut came so early in the fight. It opened in the fourth and the injury was worsened in the next round. By the seventh the referee decided he had seen enough and stepped in. The McGowan camp argued that the cut was not dangerous and the boxer should have been allowed to continue. There were hopes of a third encounter, but it was not to be. In any case, the cuts problem would not have gone away and would probably have again proved the Scot's downfall.

Earlier, McGowan had scored a surprise win in 1966 over Alan Rudkin, the British and Commonwealth bantamweight champion. Rudkin had come to prominence when he had taken the titles from the former World champion from Belfast, John Caldwell. This time he was on the receiving end, although it was a controversial points decision.

Two years later, McGowan's tenure of the titles in the heavier division was ended as Rudkin gained revenge in a contest at Manchester's Belle Vue Stadium. It was again a points decision.

McGowan had six victories over foreign opponents in the next 18 months, but was thwarted in his attempts to get a title chance. Rudkin had decided twice was enough with the Scotsman and found alternative opponents.

McGowan was often quoted as saying: "It's just as important to be a success in life as it is in boxing, maybe more so." He had shed enough blood for boxing. His retirement at the age of 27 took many by surprise.

In fact, an injury in training had prompted his decision to quit. While out doing road work he was running up a hill backwards when he felt a pain in his heel. The tendon damage required surgery and although he returned to the ring, the injury recurred.

He fought on, but the damage had taken the edge off his speed and he was getting hit with the sort of punches he would have instinctively avoided a few years earlier. "I decided to say goodbye while I could still write my name and address," he said.

Afterwards it was the familiar story. At a boxing function where he was presenting the prizes, McGowan, until then teetotal, was given a brandy and ginger ale. At first he nearly choked but he carried on and, as he admits, that was him hooked.

The fact that he had entered the licensed trade like so many other boxers on his retirement also did not help and he was soon spending too much time on the wrong side of the bar. The business ended a failure. "As I was drinking the brandy, I did not know what day it was much of the time."

His reasons behind the descent into drink are mirrored by many other boxers. "I was tied up and locked away for 17 or 18 years. Suddenly at the end of the boxing, I'm set free. What am I supposed to do?" He was unlikely to keep to the same regime imposed when he was in training as a boxer.

He now trains up-and-coming boxers and is also in demand on the after-dinner speaking circuit and as a guest at boxing evenings. As he says, he has become one of the guys at ringside who used to watch him do his job as a boxer.

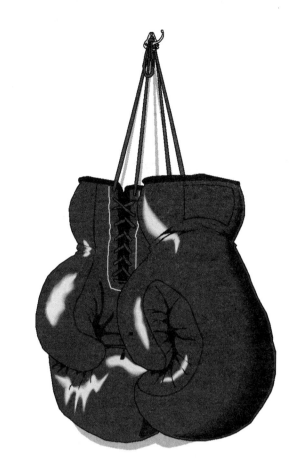

Chapter Seven

Eddie's Boys

WITH the retirement of Howard Winstone, his trainer Eddie Thomas was not yet finished with the fight game. From his stable of boxers was to emerge a World champion and a contender who took the title holder to a draw. Thomas was aware that he needed to replenish the cupboard and find a talent to match that of the home-grown boy Howard Winstone. His first hopes were that it would be another fighter from the valleys of South Wales.

In the event he was advised to consider a boxer making a huge name for himself in the amateur ring, but who hailed far from Thomas's homeland. It would be Thomas, though, who guided Ken Buchanan, the carpenter from Edinburgh, to the pinnacle of world boxing.

Buchanan was to follow in the footsteps of those other great East Coast boxers Hugh Roddin and James 'Tancy' Lee who had dominated British boxing just after the turn of the century. But he would go one better and be the first man from Edinburgh to lift a World title. Indeed, in the eyes of many, the ring exploits of Buchanan make him the greatest post-war British boxer and his record can be favourably compared to any of the all-time greats.

Buchanan achieved the seemingly impossible when he travelled to San Juan, Puerto Rico, on 26 September 1970, to take on Ismael Laguna, the champion from Panama. He would be the first Briton in 55 years to win a championship abroad. In temperatures of well over 100 degrees, he gained a split decision over 15 rounds and went on to dominate the lightweight division for two years. "It was," believes Jim Reynolds, boxing correspondent of the *Glasgow Herald*, "probably the greatest fight by a Scottish boxer."

Buchanan was an outstanding amateur champion in a career that started when, at the age of eight, he fought in the 3st 7lbs division at his local club. Two bouts later he was the champion and his career was under way. There was a scramble for his signature on a professional contract. Thomas was a great believer that an ABA title gave a young fighter a head start in the paid ranks and after seeing the Scot had no doubt that he had the makings of a champion.

True, there were flaws that would need to be ironed out. Buchanan had a habit of lifting his left foot off the floor every time he went to lead 'like he was doing the Scottish highland fling,' according to Thomas. Tommy Buchanan had overheard the comment and came over. He thought Thomas was the right man. It is easy to spot the good points in a fighter but the secret of a good trainer is to see the flaws and know how to right them.

There was also strong competition to sign Buchanan from Bobby Neill, a fellow townsman of Buchanan's from Edinburgh, who had been British featherweight champion and now headed one of the country's brightest young stables. However, Neill wanted the young Buchanan to move to London while Thomas, the other front runner, was content to let him stay in his home city and come to Wales only for training. The other factor in Thomas's favour was the success he was enjoying with Howard Winstone.

The Scot choose Thomas as his manager because his jab and move style was similar to Winstone's. He enjoyed his sparring with the man who had been World champion. "He was a marvellous boxer. It was really about who could outfox who," he remembers.

Thus it was Thomas who travelled to Edinburgh to clinch the deal. The agreement was that Buchanan should do all his training in Wales. In the ring at least the partnership was a success with 33 straight wins. The only defeat while he was under the tutelage of Thomas came when the manager reluctantly agreed to allow him to train in Edinburgh. He was defeated in a European title bout by Miguel Velazquez in Madrid.

Buchanan had done enough to get the verdict, but it had been a below par performance. Thomas believes those in charge of him at the Edinburgh gym had taken too much weight off and brought him into the contest well under the stipulated 9st 9lbs limit. His strength has been sweated out of him.

Winstone admits that some of the sparring sessions between the two turned into wars, which was only to be expected when fighters of that quality, both with a great belief in themselves, clash. Thomas himself believed a little bit of needle was not a bad thing as it kept those who fate had destined to be champions and future champions, and therefore a little bit of a breed apart, on their mettle.

The manager recalled: "He had his faults. He wasn't a nice fellow but a hell of a good fighter. You can't take that away from him. It was hard to tell who was the better with him and Winstone. They were both terrific."

To say that Buchanan had an attitude problem was an understatement. Jim Reynolds, who knows him, said: "Kenny has a bit of a downer on everybody." An unhappy childhood had engendered a sense of persecution in the fighter and a mistrust of everybody outside his family.

Thomas guided Buchanan to the British title and was then looking for a fight with the World champion, Ismael Laguna. The champion's American agent, Dewey Fregetta, had been instructed to 'find someone Laguna was sure to beat'.

In a spectacular misjudgment it was decided that the Scot would fit the bill. And to stack the odds against him, the contest was to be in the searing afternoon heat of the open-air San Juan stadium. It needed a court injunction against the BBBC to ensure the fight went ahead. They were opposed to a WBA title fight because it was the rival WBC that was supported.

"I didn't rate Laguna as outstanding," Thomas claimed later. The title was vacant and, along with the promoter Jack Solomons, he travelled to New York to persuade the powers that be that Buchanan should be one of the challengers. If Thomas wasn't worried about Laguna, he was in a very small minority. The odds against the Scot seemed insurmountable. Reynolds recalls he had not given his countryman a chance of winning.

Buchanan remembers the dawn training runs through the palm trees and the strategy for the fight. He would box in spurts because in the heat of the afternoon it was impossible to force the fight all the time. When Laguna wanted to fight, Buchanan would go on the retreat and await his chance.

For the fight Buchanan had been allocated the corner in the worst of the sun. As the fight wore on, Thomas picked the fighter up off the stool to save his energy. The fighters started fresh every round, but by the end of each they were dead on their feet in the 100 degree-plus heat and with the humidity. Thomas rubbed Vaseline on Buchanan's face while Tommy Buchanan poured sun oil over his son's shoulders to protect him.

In the end, the Scotsman wore his Panamanian opponent down and it was the man from Edinburgh who finished the stronger. Fighting with total self-belief, he pulled off one of the great shock results of all time by taking a split decision.

There had, though, been a number of pre-fight problems. Thomas was warned that the officials were to be from the United States and it would be difficult to get a decision if the fight went the full distance.

In a cunning diplomatic move, Thomas went to the owners of the stadium where the fight was to be staged and pointed out it would reflect badly on them if it looked as though one of the fighters had been denied natural justice. He was promised it would be a fair fight and was satisfied. He could ask for no more. The following day he learnt that the officials had been changed and were now all Puerto Rican. It was a weight lifted from the minds of the Buchanan camp.

The psychology games in the lead-up to the fight did not perturb Thomas. When an observer for Laguna kept objecting to the way he was taping Buchanan's hands, he told him to leave or be thrown out. The man grabbed a pair of scissors and threatened the veteran Welshman, who merely carried on with his work, whistling as he did so. The way he handled the situation greatly impressed many of the American boxing aficionados who were in Puerto Rico for the fight.

The Scot just edged the fight and got the decision. But shortly before his death in 1997, Thomas wondered: "If they'd had their own officials would we have come away with it?" As Buchanan says, he became probably the first British boxer to win a World title and get a sun tan on the same day.

Even after his victory, the BBBC hesitated in recognising him as World champion because it was the WBA version of the crown, but Buchanan had become the people's champion with his glorious performance and there was little they could do.

To underline Buchanan's credentials as champion, Thomas stayed in the United States. The Scot's talents astounded the Americans with the sheer hard quality of his fighting. His weakness, though, like that of his fellow Scottish World champion, Walter McGowan, was his vulnerability to cuts.

Thomas arranged a fight with the highly-regarded new talent Donato Paduano. The Canadian was undefeated and was a welterweight, which meant Buchanan was giving away a large weight advantage. Thomas, though, stressed the importance of fighting a heavier boxer at this time. It meant that Buchanan's lightweight title, for which he was still struggling to achieve recognition by the powers that be, was not at stake. Even if he lost he would have kept his crown. Eddie Thomas could never understand why some of his critics could not realise that.

If there were the beginnings of the rift between boxer and manager that would eventually see them part, it was this victory that convinced everybody that here was a true champion.

Indeed, it can be argued with some force that Buchanan was probably more highly regarded in the United States than in Britain. On the other side of the Atlantic, British champions are rarely rated unless they can prove themselves against America's best *and* in the United States. Only five British fighters have won World titles in America this century.

Buchanan's efforts in Puerto Rico rank alongside that and the Scotsman then did the next best thing by taking two tough fights in what was the world's leading boxing arena, Madison Square Garden in New York.

To keep the BBBC happy and further underline his credentials as one of the all-time British greats, the Scot then unified the title in a decider for the vacant WBC crown. The fight was staged in another hostile environment. This time Las Vegas.

Unlike Scottish World champions before and after him, Buchanan never fought a World title fight on his native soil. Jim Reynolds believes it was a great regret for the fighter that he never enjoyed a night boxing in front of his home supporters with the ultimate prize at stake.

As World champion, Buchanan's contract with Thomas as his manager was extended for another three years, but there were problem and one of the most publicised feuds in boxing was beginning to unfold. The Buchanan-Thomas partnership was strained, but still together in a bid to unite the title and win undisputed recognition as World lightweight champion.

In Los Angeles, Buchanan won a split decision over 15 rounds against Ruben Navarro. Seven months later, in September 1971, Buchanan faced a return with Ismael Laguna. The venue was to be Madison Square Garden and the American audience were to be treated to another 24-carat performance from the Scot.

It was this fight that also established Thomas's reputation as a brilliant corner man. Although Buchanan won comfortably in the end, on a points decision, it was the skill of the Welshman in handling cuts to both the boxer's eyes that kept him in the fight. The details, though, are not for the squeamish.

Early on, Laguna thumbed the Scot in the eye and it began to swell so badly that he was struggling to see out of it. Fortunately the damage was underneath the eye and Thomas sent for a razor blade kept in his bag in the dressing room. After a battle to get through the Madison Square Garden crowd, the blade duly arrived and Thomas cut the swelling and squeezed the blood out, keeping the swelling down and the eye open. The strictly illegal manoeuvre meant he was able to keep the wound bleeding throughout the fight.

Buchanan remembers being told by his trainer to hold on to the ropes in the corner. He was puzzled because he normally rested between rounds with his arms at his side. Then he was cut. It was, he says with understatement, a shock. But that was not all. Buchanan's other eye had also been cut and this was the more serious wound. It was a deep cut between the lid and the brow and a careful inspection of the injury would have led the doctor to call a halt to proceedings.

So on the three occasions the doctor was called to the corner, Thomas showed the weeping wound on the other eye and jammed his thumb deep into the second wound to stop the bleeding. Such cool thinking in the heat of a bout is the hallmark of a great cornerman

Thomas was proud of a report the following day in the *New York Daily News* about how he had saved the fight for Buchanan. "It was a cracking bout and he won it comfortably. After the fight he was full of appreciation."

His gratitude was shortlived. Buchanan, although a great fighter, was in the words of Thomas, 'a bloody headache'. It was not long before the Scot had found fault with his trainer and manager in a relationship that was soon to go rapidly downhill.

Buchanan needed a doctor to stitch his wounds. Thomas took him to a doctor recommended by the boxing commission who put 12 stitches in the wounds. Tommy Buchanan complained later that his son should have gone to hospital.

"The guy was the best man in New York," Thomas explained, "yet he made a lot of fuss. There was no mention of the work I had done to save the fight for him. Cut eyes are part of this job. I was proud of the job I'd done."

According to Tommy Buchanan, Ken's father, the talents of Thomas in the corner could not be questioned. He said: "Eddie was a great corner man: efficient, cool and good at assessing an opponent's strengths. There was none better. There is no way I would interfere with Eddie in the corner."

However, Buchanan senior is not as complimentary about Thomas's handling of his son outside the ring. And in his later years Thomas seems to give some validity to this when he regarded the promotion and managing side of the business as the one he would have preferred to delegate.

Tommy Buchanan cites the fight with Paduano as one where he has misgivings about the role of Thomas as

One of Merthyr's boxing legends, Eddie Thomas, a British and European welterweight champion who went on to manage two World champions.

Freddie Gilroy and Alphonse Halimi at the weigh-in for their World bantamweight fight at Wembley, with Jack Solomons.

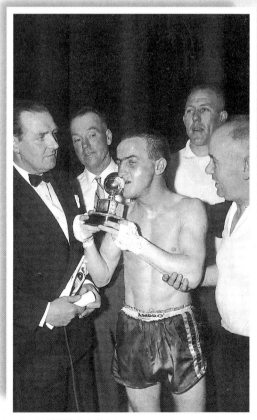

John Caldwell kisses the trophy after beating Alphonse Halimi to become World bantamweight champion.

Watched by manager Eddie Thomas (left) and promoter Harry Levene, Howard Winstone signs the contract for his World featherweight fight against Vicente Saldivar.

Howard Winstone pokes in a left to the body of Vicente Saldivar early in their World featherweight fight at Earls Court.

Joe Gans with his son, Walter McGowan, as promoter Jack Solomons holds the little Scot's arm high. He has just outpointed Salvatore Burruni to win the World flyweight title.

Ken Buchanan became British lightweight champion when he knocked out Maurice Cullen at the Anglo-American Sporting Club.

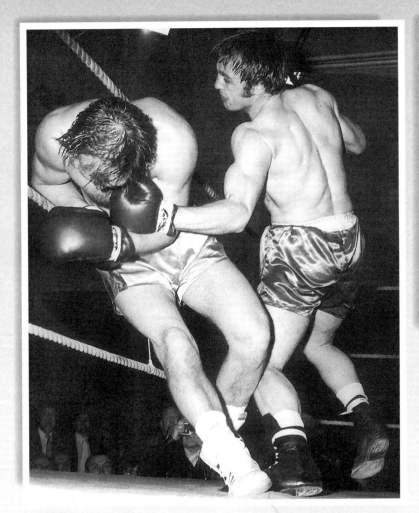

Charlie Nash, the tough Belfast lightweight who stalked Jim Watt.

Danny McAlinden smashes a left uppercut into Jack Bodell's face as he become the first Irishman to win the British heavyweight title.

Glasgow-born Jim Watt celebrates after one of his five World title wins in his home city.

Johnny Owen, proudly draped in the Welsh flag, pictured at Heathrow en route to Los Angeles and his fateful World bantamweight fight against Lupe Pinter.

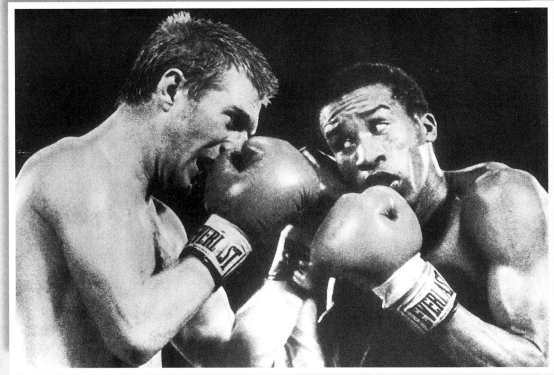

Colin Jones connects with a left hook to the cheek of Milton McCrory in the seventh round of their fight for the WBC welterweight title.

Barry McGuigan has Danilo Cabrera in trouble in Dublin. The fight ended in the 14th round and McGuigan had retained his World title.

Robbie Regan in action against France's Francis Ampufo at York Hall.

James Murray on the offensive during his fateful bout with Drew Docherty in the Grand Ballroom of the Holiday Inn in Glasgow's city centre for the British bantamweight title.

Steve Robinson on his way to a sensational World featherweight title victory over John Davison.

With only seconds of the final round to go, James Murray is in serious trouble. Two days later the boxer's life support machine was switched off and supporters of boxing again began to search their consciences.

Steve Collins has Chris Eubank in trouble during their World WBO super-middleweight fight in Cork.

Return of a champion. Steve Collins is mobbed by happy Dubliners after his victory over Eubank.

Steve Collins on his way to stopping Nigel Benn in six rounds in Manchester.

manager and his failure to deal with basics like the weight of the opponent.

Buchanan says: "Teddy Brenner, the Madison Square Garden matchmaker, Eddie Thomas and I were standing in a lift going up to the Madison Square Garden when Brenner said: 'By the way, Tommy, there will be a few pounds difference between your boy and Paduano.'

"I asked Brenner: 'What do you mean by a few pounds?' And all the time I was watching Eddie Thomas out of the corner of my eye. He was the manager. He should have spoken up. But he said nothing. Well it turned out that Ken was spotting Paduano nearly a stone by the time they entered the ring.

"Although he won and produced one of his best performances, I still think Eddie was taking too high a risk spotting that weight."

Also, Thomas was at loggerheads with the main figures who controlled the big London promotions, so Buchanan fought many of his early contests in private clubs like the National Sporting Club at the Café Royal where the purses were much smaller.

It meant that Buchanan did not have the widespread exposure his talent deserved and consequently played a part in him not winning the popular acclaim he felt he deserved when winning the World title. Indeed, after winning the British title from Maurice Cullen in February 1968, there was a wait of 18 months while the British Boxing Board of Control struggled to find him an opponent in a division not overly blessed with home-ground talent.

In 1969 it had prompted Buchanan to threaten to hand back his Lonsdale Belt and return to his trade as a carpenter rather than continue to receive the sort of money he was earning as a British champion. After the Laguna return, Thomas claimed, the boxer continually made statements to the press and in particular reporters who seemed to have the interests of some of his management rivals at heart. Buchanan was now in big demand and offers were being made to leave Thomas.

The manager considered suing one or two newspapers but reasoned that in the end 'only the lawyers win'. Buchanan was still under contract to him but there were legal problems that were costing Thomas money and the boxer was, in his words, 'starting to play ducks and drakes' in playing him off against rivals.

Thomas decided he did not want any more. "I said to him: 'Son, I've got a bit of pride, I'm Welsh.' I told him to clear off and whatever he did after that was up to him. I gave him away."

Reports at the time attributed the Thomas-Buchanan split to money. According to Tommy Buchanan the real reason was rather different.

He said: "There was a misunderstanding. It was a shame really. Eddie heard that I had applied for a license to manage. Actually it was to handle my other son, Alan, but Eddie jumped to the wrong conclusion that I was trying to take over. I wasn't. So that's what finally brought about the split.

"But I still feel that if Eddie could have negotiated as well as he handled Ken's corner during fights, then there would have been no problem."

However, Alex Morrison, a Glasgow manager and promoter, thinks Buchanan was well managed under Thomas and if Buchanan was now financially broke, it was better to look closer to home.

"Buchanan blames everybody for his troubles in the

world except himself," he believes, adding: "Whoever had managed him, Buchanan would have finished up as he is today. He never takes responsibility upon himself."

In 1975, the British boxing press conducted a poll to select the best British boxer to have emerged since 1945 and the winner was Ken Buchanan. He was the undefeated British lightweight champion from 1968 to 1971, undefeated European champion in 1974-75, and the World lightweight champion from 1970 to 1972. His place as one of the greatest fighters in boxing history should have been assured.

His WBA title was lost in controversial circumstances to one of the great champions, Roberto Duran. Buchanan claimed he was hit by a low blow and the photographic evidence appears to bear out his claim. But although there was sympathy for the Scot, his title had gone. There was one more World title fight for Buchanan, who attempted to take the crown from Guts Ishimatsu of Japan. He lost on points and his days on the world stage were over.

Then it was back to the domestic and European scene. He faced his countryman and future World champion, Jim Watt, in January 1973 and easily outpointed him for the British title he was to twice relinquish in his career. The win earned him his Lonsdale Belt outright. When offered a return with Watt, he preferred to give up the title to concentrate on the European crown. He had three successful defences of his title before retiring in 1975.

Like so many fighters before him, Ken Buchanan resumed his career. In 1979 he lost a points decision to the up-and-coming Northern Irish fighter Charlie Nash in Copenhagen. With his money gone, along with the best of his talent, he boxed on. He was unwilling to walk away gracefully, but the defeats mounted. On 24 November 1980, he was paid barely

£1,500 to box Lance Williams on the undercard at Wembley Arena, and was judged to have lost narrowly after eight punishing rounds.

At the back of the hall, Eddie Thomas turned away, no longer able to look. "Damn it man, I couldn't watch Kenny out there. I kept turning away, wanting to run from it. Fighters should be protected from themselves. The trouble is they don't thank you for telling them when to quit. I've had my share of that."

The former World lightweight champion had become just another fighter in the ring and it was painful for those who had known him at his peak.

He was booked to fight in Nigeria the following month, hoping that a decent purse would help him to buy into a public house. But it was not just the money that drove the Scot on. It was also the sense that boxing had channelled his fight against the injustices of life as he perceived them and his days of using the ring to vent his anger and frustration were drawing to a close. Recurring financial problems forced him back into the ring again, this time on the unlicensed circuit. The National Sporting Club offered to stage a benefit night to raise cash for him and thereby spare him the humiliation and physical risk of boxing on unlicensed shows.

The offer was rejected as Buchanan's pride demanded that he earn the cash himself in the only way he knew how. With his fists.

With his marriage having broken up and a defeat in the courts in an attempt to get access to his children, the ring gave him the chance to work out a lot of the aggression that was within him.

At the age of 39 and with a couple of wins on the

unlicensed circuit, it was time to call a halt. He is today planning to leave his native Scotland, unhappy that he was never given the recognition he feels he deserved. He remembers winning the Sportsman of the Year award and going to dancing lessons to prepare for taking to the floor with Princess Ann. Yet in Scotland he did not even come in the top three for their sportsman of the year title.

Dr Robin Jones, a lecturer at Brunel University who has made a study of the unlicensed boxing circuit, remarks on how sad it is that someone of Buchanan's stature should have finished up on the unlicensed circuit. With the lack of adequate safeguards and the need to keep the action high for the spectators, it is more dangerous for the boxers. And he believes it also says something of the nature of the sport in society. "Once a boxer's career is over, there are very few options left. The illegal circuit is one."

To this day, Buchanan is bitter about those who manage and promote in boxing. He believes young fighters, mainly from working-class backgrounds, are still being exploited. Practitioners of his profession are grossly underpaid.

"Boxers kill themselves in training," he says. "They have to watch their weight, not go out with women, not drink or smoke while the managers can do what they want. Managers and promoters have ruined boxing."

He has seen a couple of young lads turn professional and then struggle to get fights. The manager often has too many fighters and the trainer does not have the time which is needed to bring a boxer on. "I'm sorry to see some of the younger boxers with ability, but nobody to bring it out."

Looking back on his career, he reflects: "I was Edinburgh's first boxing World champion but they never did anything for me. Not even a meal. If I had been a Wimbledon tennis champion then it would have been different." And he adds: "Throughout my life I have had to fight for anything I wanted and I still have to do that now."

—oOo—

Before their relationship ended in rancorous dispute, Eddie Thomas had taken Buchanan to the World title. Thomas was mapping out a similar route for Colin Jones, the Welsh welterweight from Gorseinon, who went on to fight three times for the World championship. Jones was born on 21 March 1959. After a glittering amateur career which included representing Britain at the Olympic Games, he left his local boxing club at Penyrheol and signed professional forms with Thomas.

The veteran trainer had been told about the abilities of Jones while he was still boxing in the schoolboy ranks and had asked a boxing acquaintance to keep a close eye on his progress. Thomas received the call that the youngster was ready.

Jones was an eager pupil, following Thomas's instructions and learning quickly. After Buchanan, his new fighter was easy to handle. "If I said something he'd try it. He was great."

And while once a fighter's career is over there is normally a parting of the ways, Thomas and Jones remained close. The boxer was a regular visitor at the home of his former manager as he fought the disease that was to take his life and he has nothing but praise for his mentor.

Jones's ability to take out opponents with one punch made him a box office hit from the outset. Eleven straight wins brought him a British title eliminator against Joey Mack, who was dispatched in the tenth round as Jones earned himself a title fight.

Thomas decided to give Jones a final warm-up before he challenged Kirkland Laing for the British belt and he chose the experienced Cardiff boxer, Billy Waith, to provide the opposition. The resulting fight at the World Sporting Club in Mayfair, London, was shrouded in controversy with Waith constantly complaining that Jones was hitting him in the kidneys. After the fight, Waith appeared to prove his case with a large swelling at the base of his spine. Thomas always insisted that Waith was knocked-out with two legitimate left hooks to the stomach.

The British welterweight championship fight between the champion Laing and challenger Jones created tremendous excitement. It had everything necessary for a great fight with a mighty puncher against a dazzling boxer and both men were undefeated.

The contest is still remembered as one of the all-time great British title fights. Laing won each of the first eight rounds — indeed it was round three before Jones landed a punch.

It took only 30 seconds, however, for Jones to take the title. The Welshman threw a huge right which landed flush on the champion's jaw as his gumshield landed in the third row.

Laing clung to the top rope and stayed on his feet. Cutting loose with both hands, Jones hammered blows at the now-defenceless Laing and was soon the new welterweight champion of Great Britain.

Jones took the Commonwealth title by beating the Guyanese Mark Harris before sustaining his first defeat — a disqualification by referee Adrian Morgan for hitting American Curtis Ramsey while he was on the floor. Four more victories, all inside a total of ten rounds, including one Commonwealth defence and a European title fight, and

Jones got his big chance. A fight for the vacant WBA World welterweight championship.

When Sugar Ray Leonard gave up the title, Jones was given the opportunity to fight the American Milton McCrory. According to the bookmakers, the unbeaten McCrory was the 7-1 on favourite.

Jones chased the retreating American throughout the fight but had to be satisfied with a draw. José Suliman of the World Boxing Council immediately sanctioned a re-match.

Five months after the first battle, McCrory versus Jones took place in Las Vegas on 13 August 1983. It was a magnificent fight throughout the 12 rounds. Jones was on the canvas in the first but recovered to hurt McCrory on several occasions before the American won the split decision.

Colin Jones was to make one more attempt for the World crown against one of the all-time greats, Don Curry. Jones's face was cut to pieces in four brutal rounds. He never fought again, retiring without a World title, but with a great deal of money.

Thomas had hoped to put Jones against an ageing Curry who was struggling to make the weight. His judgement was out but, he believed, not by much.

The following year, in a surprise victory, Britain's Lloyd Honeyghan stopped the great champion in six rounds. Thomas commented: "No disrespect to Honeyghan, but he was never the fighter that Colin Jones was."

—oOo—

Another of Thomas's achievements during the 1970s was to make Danny McAlinden the first Irishman to win the British heavyweight title. They called him 'Dangerous Dan' and 'Dynamite Dan' as he mowed down a succession of heavyweights, with just a few stumbles along the way to win the British championship.

Then, as his career hit the skids and he made a series of disastrous comebacks, Dan McAlinden of Newry, County Down, became known as 'Desperate Dan.' Unlike the comic book character, McAlinden did not have a chin of steel. He could be tagged with alarming ease and he was knocked down or stopped eight times in 45 professional contests. Domestic and managerial troubles did not help his concentration at the height of his career.

The paths of Danny McAlinden and the great Welsh trainer Eddie Thomas crossed at Madison Square Garden. His opponent in New York was Rahman Ali, whose brother, Mohammed Ali, was top of the bill against Joe Frazier. In a war of words, Thomas urged McAlinden to ask his opponent which corner he wanted knocking down in. "That got Ali going," recalled the manager, who enjoyed another good night at the Garden after his success with Buchanan.

It was the night the better-known of the Alis had his self-proclaimed invincibility shattered by the pounding fists of Frazier. McAlinden made it an especially bad night for the Ali clan with a convincing victory over Rahman. The bout was just before the main event and as McAlinden and Thomas left the ring, they heard a shout. "Just a minute, I want to see the man who just whupped my little brother," said Ali, who started clowning around and sparring up to the Irishman.

Not sure of McAlinden's name, he snarled: "I'm going to whup you, MacMillan, for what you done to my brother." McAlinden confidently retorted: "I can beat you just as I did your brother." Later Ali expressed a desire to deliver a lesson to the Irishman for being too cocky, but their ringside war of words was as close as they ever got, which was perhaps just as well for McAlinden.

Thomas returned to McAlinden's corner for a crack at Jack Bodell's British and Commonwealth heavyweight championships. It was all over in two rounds with the champion lying face down on the canvas. Unfortunately, the promotion was poorly supported as it was on the same evening that Buchanan fought Roberto Duran for the World title. Under different circumstances Thomas would have been not in Birmingham but in the corner of his former protégé in Madison Square Garden.

What should have been an enjoyable and lucrative career for the new heavyweight champion turned out to be a sorry tale of missed chances, out-of-the-ring problems and shock defeats. McAlinden did not have the crowd-pulling potential to attract fights at the higher level and needed a contest with Joe Bugner, the European champion, to gain some credibility and the chance of a few big-money purses. But after a long wait, his chance slipped by when he was injured in a warm-up fight for the big contest with Bugner and a £100,000 fight night. The fight was off and while Bugner went on to meet Ali and Frazier, the Irishman slipped towards obscurity.

A broken thumb led to a proposed title fight with Bunny Johnson being postponed for the first time. An illness forced a second cancellation. Finally, before an audience of under 1,000 in January 1975, McAlinden was counted out in the ninth. He lost a title challenge against Richard Dunn and as his career declined, the low point came as McAlinden was booed into a Derry ring. Part of the reason for the crowd's hostility was undoubtedly the boxer's widely publicised break-up with his wife, Patricia.

He had been fined £100 by Coventry magistrates after pleading guilty to maliciously wounding his wife and another man after tracing them to a nightclub.

His problems have continued to this day. Early in 1997 he was jailed for three months after a drunken attack on a waiter in an Indian restaurant in London's East End. McAlinden, 48, had smashed a chair over the waiter's head. He admitted affray. In his defence the court Southwark Crown Court was told the boxer had beaten a long battle against drink.

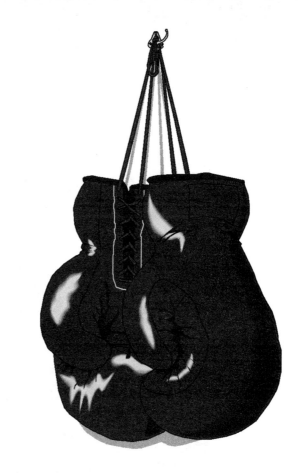

Chapter
Eight

Nash and Watt and the Sectarian Divide

AS Ken Buchanan's star waned, a boxer from Glasgow whose chance seemed to have passed him by was to become the next Celtic World champion. He was helped by an English manager, Terry Lawless, with the contacts to ensure Jim Watt reached the top.

In Watt's success lies a profound irony, not that irony is anything new in the fight game. Max Schmeling, for example, was trumpeted by the Nazis as a classic example of Aryan manhood yet in Joe Jacobs he had a Jewish manager.

Watt, the proud Glaswegian, the Scotsman whose deep national pride led him to lead a stirring rendition of *Flower of Scotland* after his World title win over American Howard Davis at Ibrox Park, is perhaps one of the finest examples in support of Dr Samuel Johnson's belief that 'the noblest prospect a Scotsman ever sees is the High Road to England'. For it was in Romford, Essex, not Ruchill, Glasgow, that Watt found his fistic saviour. It saw Watt turn from a boxer exhilarated to receive £4,200 for his losing championship battle with Buchanan in 1973 into the recipient of more than 100 times as much for the Davis contest.

There are those, however, who will argue that without Glasgow and the fervour of his hometown fans, Watt would never have held the World lightweight title for the two years that he did. As Lawless said of Watt's defence against Roberto Vasquez: "He was beaten by the bagpipes before he entered the ring."

Watt has not forgotten the debt he owes to James 'Careful' Murray, the manager who discovered Watt when he first arrived at his Glasgow gym because bad weather had scuppered the football and the youngster had nothing to do.

"I had seen an advert on a wall and I went along to see what it was like," recalls Watt, "I was trying a range of sports and had no great ambitions to be a boxer. Nobody can choose what they are good at and I just happened to be good at boxing."

The 'choir boy' looks still enjoyed by the former champion can be directly attributed to Murray's early and often stern refusal to throw Watt to the wolves for a few pounds of pecuniary gain.

Watt remembers how good Murray was to him in those early days. Both Murray and Lawless were father figures to the boxer, whose own father died at a young age. And it was the death of his father when he was seven that Watt believes had the biggest impact on his character, forcing him to be responsible and gain a degree of independence. He had to grow up quickly.

"I remember from an early age with my mother at work, I had a key to the door tied around my neck," he said, "I knew from a younger age than most to look after myself and not ask for too many favours from anybody else."

Murray filled an important void in his world and the disciplined life that goes with boxing suited him. Although they were to later part company, Watt has nothing but praise for his former manager.

"Throughout my boxing career I only had two managers looking after my affairs. I was with Jim Murray for 12 years and he always looked after me properly and didn't put me into fights I shouldn't have been in," he says.

But however important Murray's influence was in the early years, without Lawless the boxer would have disappeared without trace. As it was, Watt got out of boxing with his looks and bank balance intact. He defended his title four times, eventually losing it to the legendary Mexican, Alexis Arguello. He then retired and became a successful boxing commentator as well as pursuing business interests outside the sport. Watt has proved one of the few exceptions to the Celtic rule.

The boxer himself has his own theories about why this was so. His upbringing had taught him the value of money, but perhaps more importantly he found fame and glory late in life for a boxer. By the time the big pay days arrived, he had already set up his own business and was married with a family. He admits that if the fortune had presented itself five or more years before it did, he probably would not have been able to cope.

Unlike many boxers before him, he also had the sense to realise that the big fights were not going to last forever. Particularly not for a man who was 31 when he won the championship. By then he was well past the sell-by date for the majority of boxers.

"I had the sense to realise that I had moved into a false position in my life," he says today. "I knew it wasn't going to last forever and I had to exploit the opportunity and set myself up for life."

He also believes that sportsmen, particularly those from working-class sports like boxing, are not prepared for life after their careers end. All their energies have been focused on honing their talents as athletes. Their family background tends to mean there is no sensible advice thereafter on what to do with the cash as it rolls in. "It's not that the boxer is daft or anything, just that he is not prepared for the position he finds himself in."

Watt believes the nature of the Celt may also be a factor. He says Celts are passionate people who go from one extreme to another. Boxers who as sportsmen gave it everything will then give their full attention to taking a few drinks if that is what they decide to do. He laments that drive is rarely channelled into business where they would make millions. Instead boxers who have been deprived of a lot of things enjoyed by the rest of society because of training for their sport, think they have a lot of catching up to do. It tends to prove their downfall.

Watt's own boxing success is all the more remarkable because he was not a natural enthusiast of the sport and admits that in his youth he gave it up a few times to return to playing soccer. The persuasive Murray was always on hand, though, to lure him back. "I probably needed more encouragement than most," says Watt.

It was in 1963 that the 14-year-old Watt first arrived at the Cardowan Boxing Club and showed enough aptitude to attract Murray's attention, coupled with a willingness to learn.

Murray did not rush the newcomer but guided him carefully through the amateur ranks that saw him represent Scotland and in 1968 win the British ABA championships. He was selected to represent Britain in the Mexico Olympics, but Murray decided it was time for him to turn professional. It was not the first time in Watt's career that the paternalistic Murray had made what appeared curious decisions. He had pulled his young fighter out of international meets in the past because he could not be accommodated in the Scotland coaching set up and would be unable to keep an eye on his protégé from his corner.

He also had firm ideas on what was the right preparation for boxers. To Watt's embarrassment he once created a scene and sent back the meal being enjoyed by the rest of the Scottish squad because he considered it inappropriate. He insisted his fighter was brought an omelette instead.

Yet the manager's decisions were always what he thought were in Watt's best interests. And in the boxer's early days when his enthusiasm for the sport was not absolute, he rightly erred on the side of caution. A bad beating could have been boxing's loss and a local park soccer side's gain.

Watt's career in the paid ranks started well enough. His first professional fight was at Hamilton Town Hall against the London-based Nigerian Santos Martins The Second. Watt won with a fourth round knock-out. His career moved on apace and he won a final eliminator for the British title held by Ken Buchanan against Willie Reilly when the referee stopped the contest because of a badly cut eye.

But after Buchanan relinquished the title, the two fought again and this time it was Reilly who emerged the victor in an early setback in the young Scot's career. A seventh-round clash of heads left Watt with a deep cut at the side of his right eye. The referee gave him a few rounds, but as the cut worsened, he stopped the contest in the tenth.

Watt emerged from the fight with nine stitches and Reilly with the British championship. However, he was to resign it in bizarre fashion, refusing to fight for what he believed was a derisory purse. The decision of Reilly was to prove a portent for Watt early in his career. British boxing was in the doldrums. Outside the London fights sewn up by a clique of promoters and managers, decent pay days were hard to come by.

The frustration Reilly felt manifest itself in his walking away from the fight game. Watt stuck with it but in the next couple of years under Murray he would fully understand the sentiments.

In the meantime, the man from Glasgow had his chance and in a fight for the title declared vacant by the British Boxing Board of Control he fought Tony Riley on 3 May 1972, and legendary referee Harry Gibbs stopped the fight in the 12th. The purse for Watt's efforts was £1,806.

With Buchanan's defeat against Roberto Duran stripping him of his World title, the former champion returned to the domestic scene with a vengeance. Watt was forced to make a mandatory defence and although past his prime, Buchanan was a difficult opponent for a first defence. And so it proved. Buchanan had his countryman down in the first and although

Watt survived to lose a points decision, it was a huge margin against him. The champion appeared overawed by the man with the glorious past and it was a disappointing performance.

Watt's own future triumphs appeared light years away. Murray's lack of contacts with those running the major promotions and his abrasive character that was inclined to antagonise people meant Watt struggled to get meaningful fights with decent purses.

In desperation there was a sojourn in South Africa in 1974 where he won a couple of fights before returning to contest a British title eliminator against the Welshman, Billy Waith, in Caerphilly, South Wales, in a contest where Eddie Thomas was the matchmaker.

Watt had travelled to South Africa on his own and this probably reinforced the idea that he could manage his later career on his own. For a man who had had responsibility thrust on him at the age of seven, such a move was not daunting. A points win over Waith gave Watt another chance at Buchanan, the man Thomas formerly managed and who had taken Watt's British title. However, it was never to be, with the former World champion seeking bigger prizes on the European trail.

Watt did regain the British title, beating Johnny Cheshire in January 1975, but it would be two years before he defended his crown. With his career in the doldrums he embarked on an unsuccessful foreign campaign. He lost a Commonwealth title fight against Jonathan Dele in Lagos, Nigeria, on points in a contest Murray was unwise to take. Hotel and training conditions were poor and there was a hostile crowd supporting the local man.

What proved a much worse blow, though, was the defeat in a contest for the European lightweight title vacated after

Buchanan's retirement, against the Frenchman Andre Holyk in Lyon. This was the fight that brought the curtain down on his partnership with Murray. The Scot's accurate southpaw jab appeared to have given him a commanding lead, but he had been unable to finish the tiring Frenchman and relying on the judges in Continental fights can be a risky business. The judges duly underlined why, giving Holyk the title on the split decision.

For a career that had taken a lot of knocks the disappointment of this defeat was too much. Watt believes he was 'robbed' of the European championship in a disgraceful decision by the judges. "With that I thought my chance had gone," he admits.

After 12 years, it was the end of the road for the partnership between Murray and Watt. A telephone call was all it took. Murray wanted £500 because there was still a year of the contract left to run. Watt refused and that was it.

Watt admits that he thought, at 27, his career was now virtually over. All he wanted to do was perhaps pick up a few half-decent pay days defending his British title before retiring, and hopefully win a Lonsdale Belt outright. Little did he know that at a time when most boxers are in decline, the best for Watt was yet to come.

At this stage he had no intention of finding a new manager. He was in business on his own in the motor trade and thought he could manage his own affairs in the twilight of his career.

The call from Terry Lawless came as a surprise. The experienced manager told Watt he had always admired him as a boxer and thought he should have achieved more. The partnership was agreed and the rest is history. When Watt got his chances, he made sure he took them.

By the mid-1970s Lawless was a major figure at the height of his power. When Watt joined him he already had the World welterweight champion John H. Stracey in his stable. Lawless could open doors of opportunity which were closed to most British champions. He also worked on Watt's style. The Scot was at heart a defensive boxer. Murray had always felt he should be more aggressive, but perhaps Watt's early uncertainty about the fight game had led him to adopt a safety-first attitude.

Under his new manger he developed a more ruthless edge and was ready to unleash more powerful punches.

Throughout his career Watt was stalked by the tough Northern Ireland lightweight Charlie Nash. Thirteen straight victories as a professional placed Nash as the leading contender for Jim Watt's British lightweight title. But the Scotsman was in no hurry to accommodate him and the difficulty in getting Watt into the ring with him led Nash to fuel rumours that the Scot was afraid to face him, particularly in his home town of Derry.

The British title defence had gone out to purse offers and the highest was to stage the fight in Derry at the height of the Troubles. Watt says he was not concerned about travelling to Ireland and believed he could knock Nash out. His manager Lawless, however, was concerned that if it went the distance the officials might be intimidated. Watt does not believe this would be the case and acknowledges that the violence has never split over into sport.

With the chance of a European title fight, Watt refused to defend his British crown and the British Boxing Board of Control stripped the Glasgow man of his title. Nash won the vacant championship by beating Londoner Johnny Claydon. The Irishman now wanted the match with Watt for the European title which the Scot held. Again Watt relinquished the crown to concentrate on higher honours and Nash took it and thus consolidated his position in the World rankings.

At the age of 31, Watt now had the chance of a World title fight. The great Roberto Duran, who had ended Buchanan's reign as champion, relinquished the undisputed crown and both the WBC and WBA arranged contests for their respective titles. For the WBC title, Watt was to fight the Colombian Alfredo Pitalua in Glasgow. It was the opportunity that Watt had been waiting for all his career and he took it gratefully, knocking-out his opponent in 12 rounds.

In contrast to Buchanan — who claims his home city of Edinburgh never gave him the recognition he deserved or supported his cause — Glasgow, with its great tradition as a boxing city, did all it could to help their prospective World champion.

The fight was staged in the city, thanks to sponsorship from the city council. It was the sort of backing Buchanan must have dreamed of in Edinburgh, where they did not even manage a civic reception when he returned from Puerto Rico with the title. His reception came courtesy of a Scottish national newspaper.

The backing Watt received from his native city was not forgotten. It made sense to continue fighting at home. "It was my choice to box in Scotland. I wanted to repay Glasgow and I'm also very patriotic. I enjoyed boxing in front of Scottish supporters."

Nash's first defence of his European title was against the now ageing Ken Buchanan. Yet despite still being in decline, Nash kept his title only with a desperately close points decision.

Watt had made a successful first defence, knocking-out

Robert Vasquez in nine rounds. Now the way was paved for the dual with Watt for the WBC World title. The man from Derry was willing to go anywhere to contest the major honour. Inevitably, it meant a trip across the water to Scotland.

"Because I had been twice ordered to fight Nash and twice relinquished the title, people got this funny idea I was scared. It wasn't the case," says Watt. "It was that business dictated taking bigger fights."

And when the chance came for the Scot to make a voluntary defence, he gave Nash his chance. The fight was a memorable night for the Kelvin Hall. Newspapers had speculated there might be trouble with a Scottish Protestant fighting an Irish Catholic, but in the crowd the occasion passed off peacefully. In the ring, though, it was a brutal affair.

Nash came out strongly, looking to hurt the champion early on and make him more cautious in his attacks as the fight wore on. It worked better than anticipated with a combination of punches putting Watt on the canvas in the first round. But the Irishman's hopes were dashed when, as he pressed forward to finish off a stunned Watt, there was a clash of heads which opened a bad cut. With such an injury in the first round it meant Nash's fight plan of trying to get the older Watt to go the distance had to be scrapped. Once the referee came to the corner and said it was a bad cut, the instructions to Nash were that he had to knock-out the champion.

The task proved too tough for a boxer who lacked an explosive punch. The referee gave him a few rounds but as Nash attacked, he proved an easy target for Watt who landed a succession of punches before the fight was stopped in the fourth.

For Watt honour was settled. "Charlie Nash had been

bugging me for a long time, telling the world I was afraid to box him. It was the right thing for him to do as far as his career was concerned and there is no personal animosity between us. It was good to get Nash out of my hair once and for all."

Speaking at a Derry gym where he coaches boxing and encourages young talent, Nash not surprisingly sees things slightly differently in his relations with the man from Glasgow. As far as the Irishman is concerned he believes Watt's decision not to fight in Derry was because the home support would have given him too big an edge whichever title was at stake. It is not a view shared by local boxing journalist Dennis O'Hara of the *Belfast Newsletter*, who believes Watt's decision not to come to Derry owed more to boxing politics than sectarian troubles.

After beating Buchanan in Denmark in 1979 in a European title fight, Nash had little choice but to accept the World title chance on Watt's terms. Not only was it in Glasgow but the Irishman felt the cash on offer was not very good. At least having to travel to fight was nothing new to Nash. Virtually all his major fights were outside Northern Ireland. He believes this did much to blight his career. The Watt fight came over two years too late in his career.

The Irishman is far from modest in outlining his talents. "I was faster and more skilful than Watt, who was a strong fighter and had a harder punch. The fight ended in a disappointing way with a cut and I never got another chance."

Nash should have realised that his best fighting days were behind him. He fought on but never regained any of his titles in a series of blood-soaked defeats.

For most of his professional career Nash had to fight away from home due to the lack of promotion in a Northern

Ireland riven by the Troubles. But the conflict had a much greater affect on Nash than merely forcing him to leave his native land to fight. He came from the troubled Creggan area of Derry. His brother, Jack, was one of the 13 civilians shot dead by British troops on the infamous 'Bloody Sunday' in January 1972. His father was wounded in the same incident.

If the defeat at the hands of Watt ended Nash's hopes of remaining at the highest level in boxing, it was merely a stepping stone for the Scotsman on his way to his greatest moment of glory. He had won the WBC World title and defended it twice, yet in the eyes of many, particularly across the Atlantic, he merely had the crown on loan until the rightful owner arrived to collect it.

The heir apparent was an American fighter, Howard Davis, who had won a gold medal at the Montreal Olympic Games and was progressing slowly but purposefully in the paid ranks with 13 straight wins His performances had given voice to a few doubts about his pedigree, with only five of his wins on stoppages and a sense he might not have the required hunger for the fight game. Yet many still installed him as favourite against the champion.

Watt again had the advantage of a huge home support for the only open-air fight in his boxing career. Nearly 30,000 were at Ibrox Park, Glasgow, for the contest and there was no doubt who they were going to be cheering for. Fighting on your home patch has many advantages but there are a few drawbacks. As Watt says it is not like fighting in somewhere like Italy, where you can come back with the 'I was robbed' stories and nobody knows the truth. Everybody can see what happens with their own eyes. There is an enormous sense of expectancy on the boxer's shoulders. The pressure is on to perform well. But if in the closing rounds their fighter is flagging, the Scottish crowd can lift their man and give him renewed strength.

Nimble footwork allied to fast hands were Davis's strengths, while Watt looked to cramp him and deprive him of space. Watt's style was as a pressure boxer, always going forward and that had to be the plan. Watt remembers fans turning up wearing Scottish scarves and carrying national flags. Their roar drowned out the pipers and drums playing *Scotland the Brave* as the boxers entered the ring. It was to be another great fight night in Scotland.

It was a splendid performance from both fighters, but the Scot always had the edge. There was no knock-down but his superior work gave him a unanimous points win as well as his biggest pay day. He was a month short of his 32nd birthday.

Looking back on his championship fights in Glasgow, Watt explains that as well as being a patriotic move it also made sense from a business point of view. As well as huge attendances at the event, US television were persuaded to come to Scotland, bringing the money that generated.

He says: "I think most Scots are patriotic and it is something I look back on with pride that all my successful fights were in Scotland. Even now people still come up and tell me what they did on the day of the championship fights."

There was another successful defence, against Sean O'Grady of the United States when both fighters were badly cut but it was the American who was stopped in the 12th round with a badly gashed forehead.

The reign of Watt that had seen him come from the disappointment of his European title defeat in France to become World champion and successfully defend his title four times ended at the hands of the Nicaraguan Alexis Arguello.

Arguello had already held the WBC super-featherweight title for two years and Watt knew it would be a tough night at Wembley. He went the distance, but had no complaints about the decision. "He was better on the night and I lost it fairly clearly."

Reflecting on the end of his career, Watt says he has no regrets. It had to come to an end and he enjoyed being World champion. Particularly as for most of his career he thought it would never happen. Now, he reasoned, it was time to call it a day. There was little point going down slowly being stripped of his remaining titles. A career in boxing commentary beckoned and as he says, he had managed to stick a few quid in the bank.

Watt's place in the Scottish boxing roll of honour alongside the likes of Benny Lynch, Jackie Paterson and Walter McGowan was assured. Fighting in his home city had helped give Scotland a huge sporting lift. It was not just the skill he showed in the ring, but the dignified way he carried himself out of it. He was a great diplomat for Scotland.

The debate on who is the greatest of the Scottish World champions can occupy hours of pub time on a Saturday night. There is no doubt, though, that Watt has handled his success the best.

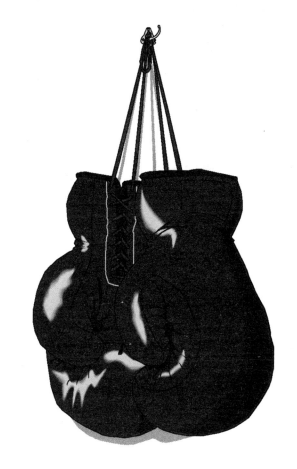

Chapter Nine

The Death of Johnny Owen

T HE sacrifices boxers have to make are many. To reach the top requires total dedication to the way of life of the professional fighter. And the hardest of sports sometimes exacts the ultimate price. So it was for Johnny Owen. The thin and frail-looking 24-year-old from Merthyr Tydfil in South Wales reached for the sport's highest honour and paid with his life.

Such fatalities inevitably strengthen the hand of those opposed to boxing. For those with a medical or moral objection, each tragedy is merely another low point in a sport they regard as basic barbarity. The fact that injuries may be greater in other sports is often touted as a defence.

Professional jockeys are more likely to sustain serious injury in a career than their counterparts in boxing. The harsh truth with boxing is that it is a gladiatorial battle that will often depend on beating an opponent senseless.

The death of Owen can be touted as a prime example, by those opposed to the sport, of why it should be ended. Yet for the supporters of boxing it offers an illustration of a man for whom boxing was everything. In the case of the death of James Murray, boxing also was the major motivation in his life. The sport transformed a tearaway into an athlete with a goal to aim for.

The reaction of his distraught parents, who in their saddest hour refused to denounce the sport, or his opponent in the fatal fight, shows they have an insight into what boxing means. And its importance to their son.

Tragedies inevitably focus the mind as it did for those involved with the deaths of Owen and Murray. But as the journalist Ken Jones explained, despite the misgivings that surface he would continue to be at ringside for the next big fight. And Johnny Owen would understand why.

Hindsight can also be a wonderful thing and there are those who recall forebodings about Owen taking on a strong champion in a hostile environment. Yet the battling boxer who devoted his life to the sport had lost only one of 26 fights and was British, Commonwealth and European champion. A World title shot was the next obvious step.

A near neighbour of Owen's in Merthyr was Howard Winstone, who fought three tough losing championship fights against the impressive Vicente Saldivar, including a daunting trip to Mexico City. Despite those reverses he was still driven to compete at the highest level for the World crown. For him, the hard work and pain paid off when he lifted the WBC featherweight championship against Mitsun-ori Seki in 1968. He understood why Owen had to take the trip to Los Angeles, the ambition that had driven the boxer throughout his career, forcing his body through the arduous training routines, assiduously learning his craft.

With genuine emotion Winstone recalls what a terrible tragedy it was when a fellow son of Merthyr died in such circumstances. How the tough valley's town had mourned one of its own and remembered the glory the man with the matchstick physique had brought. Yet he had no doubts that Owen had to take the fight. It was the sort of chance of which boxers dream — perhaps a once-only opportunity to put a line in a record book and know you were the best.

While Winstone's thoughts were with the family, there was no recrimination for Owen's trainer, Dai Gardiner. "People say he shouldn't have taken the fight, but he had to do it. Owen had to go for the title."

Owen's opponent for the fateful fight was the holder of the WBC bantamweight title Lupe Pintor. It was thought a legitimate match despite the apprehension felt by some of the Welshman's compatriots. This stemmed, in part, from the champion's obvious pedigree. A powerful fighter, he had 41 victories behind him in 48 outings and the Mexican would enjoy huge support from the largely Hispanic crowd at the Olympic Auditorium.

Owen's career had started when he joined his local boxing club at the age of ten and he went on to box for Wales as an amateur. When it came to turn professional, he signed with Dai Gardiner, who had a gym at New Tredegar, about nine miles from the boxer's home.

Boxing was his entire life. By the time he made his professional debut he still had no outside interests. He did not even have a girlfriend. Archive footage shows a shy, diffident character.

It was only when Owen ducked through the ropes that he began to express himself. Although he was tall with long skinny arms, the boxer was a more powerful puncher than his appearance would suggest and he was not averse to mixing at close quarters.

With four British title wins in a row between 1977 and 1980 and with Commonwealth and European triumphs, there was nowhere else to go but for a shot at the World title. Certainly there were few challenging or financially rewarding fights on the home front.

Owen had relieved Paddy Maguire of his British title in only his tenth fight. For becoming champion he received £7,070. Within two years he had won a Lonsdale Belt outright. He took the vacant Commonwealth title, defeating the Australian Paul Ferreri, and won the European crown from Juan Francisco Rodriguez of Spain at the second attempt after Gardiner had managed to secure the fight in South Wales. Most neutrals believe he should have had the verdict in Spain, except that does not happen. That he had competed with such a tough opponent and emerged with such credit was further ammunition for the case for taking the Pintor contest.

Owen was the natural contender for the World title and in September 1980 he travelled to Los Angeles to challenge Pintor. A small number of fans travelled with him to give him support.

The journalist Ken Jones, while not wishing to criticise Gardiner, believes corners were cut to save money in preparations for the fight. Owen arrived only a week before the contest, despite an eight-hour time difference (one day for each hour is the general rule of thumb for recovery for even ordinary travellers.) There were insufficient sparring partners and the training was not ideal for such a tough contest. The hotel was basic. For his fateful fight, Jones believes Owen fought for a purse of only around £10,000. And he admits he was apprehensive about him taking the fight.

Eddie Thomas, the veteran manager who also hailed from Merthyr, had also had his doubts about taking such a tough fight so soon in Owen's career. He would also have preferred to have got the champion to travel to London. He said: "I don't want to knock anybody in the fight game, but I did say at the time it was a bit soon and I would rather they had waited a bit longer. The Hispanics love their boxing, but they love their own fighters. I knew it was going to be tough for Owen."

He compared it with Scotland where the crowd can lift their own boxer to new heights and taking a title is never easy at the best of times, even for outstanding fighters. Thomas remembers the Winstone fight in Mexico City, where the stadium was like a cauldron.

Despite the overwhelming odds against him, most ringside observers had Owen ahead at the halfway stage in the Olympic Auditorium. The heat, though, was beginning to take its toll and the strong Mexican began to come into his own. The Welshman was knocked down in the ninth but showed great courage in rallying and, despite taking punishment, he survived until the last round.

The contest was still close enough to allow Owen to continue. This was the Welshman's bid for a World title and he deserved his chance. His trainer can lament that if only he had thrown in the towel at that stage, then the ending would have been different. But he is merely punishing himself.

There was only 40 seconds of the 12th round left when the tragic dénouement to the brave challenge of Johnny Owen arrived. A short right sent Owen to his knees and after a mandatory count he was driven to the other side of the ring and there took a savage right. He fell backwards and his head thudded against the floor. The referee stopped the fight without bothering to count. Those at ringside knew it was serious.

A local journalist, Gareth Jones, boxing correspondent with the *South Wales Echo*, recalls Owen falling 'like a marionette with its strings cut'. Slumped in his corner, the boxer was clearly in distress.

It did not matter to the crowd, who booed and spat at the fighter and his trainer as Owen was taken by stretcher in a coma from the ring. Everything in the Welshman's corner was stolen while he was being tended to. Gardiner believes the hostility was partly because the home crowd thought they were going to lose their World champion.

From Gardiner's vantage point in the corner, the fight had been going well. Although a cut in the fourth had caused some concern, they had dealt with it. Owen was boxing well and using his long reach to accumulate points. When the Welshman went down in the ninth, it was the first time in his career that he had been put on the canvas. Gardiner was concerned, but Owen had done well in the tenth and 11th rounds.

Gareth Jones has no doubt that the fighter should have been in there. It was not a mismatch. At the brutal end, one of the judges still had the Welshman ahead on points, although it was of no consolation to brave Owen. Gardiner travelled to the hospital where there was a three-hour operation to remove a blood clot from the brain. It was not until then that the trainer was made aware of just how serious was the situation. Numbed, he waited and hoped.

Owen was to linger in a coma for seven weeks. His mother had heard of his plight back home in Merthyr listening to a radio report of the fight. The family flew out to be with him. For Gardiner, the worst part was the intrusive media coverage. The family were hounded at the hospital by reporters asking the same questions for news of the boxer's progress. The sad answer was always the same. At home there were daily bulletins on his progress and in Merthyr they prayed and hoped.

Gardiner recalls the nightmare where he struggled to take in what was happening as reporters asked another barrage of questions. "I didn't know whether I was coming or going. Nothing like this had ever happened to me before. It was all so very sad."

At one stage Owen appeared to rally, but it was not to be. He died on 4 November 1980. Eddie Thomas and his wife arranged for the body to be returned from Los Angeles. It took a few hours and the intervention of the local MP to cut through bureaucratic hurdles at the airport to get the body released. On seeing the coffin at Gatwick Airport, Thomas was left to question his involvement in a sport that had been his life.

"At such times you often wonder what the hell are we doing in this game," he said. "You think of the successes, but there is more go the other way than are successful and you wonder what help they get when it is needed."

It was the nature of professional boxing that few who took part did well from it, and for some like Owen there was a high price to pay. And Thomas wondered whether it was right that boxing should be supported. He thought, though, that there was that part of man's nature, and particularly that of the Celt, to fight. He believed the battles would take place outside the ring rather than in it and that would prove far worse.

As for the risk of death and injury, it was not something he had ever considered. Just as he never considered it when he went down into the bowels of the earth as a coal miner. There was obviously danger, but it was accepted without thought.

"It's a curious thing, but although people say boxers know the dangers when going into the ring, I have never heard fighters talk about it," he said.

Gardiner remembers the funeral in a haze. The chapel was full for a traditional Valleys' service. It was a moving and emotional occasion. The town of Merthyr came to a standstill as the body was taken to be laid to rest. A male voice choir sang hymns at the cemetery. But the trainer confesses "I was in cloud cuckoo land to be honest. I just remember it being very sad."

A post mortem showed a weakness in the boxer's skull that left him susceptible to brain injury and would have prevented him taking to the ring today. Routine medical arrangements before fights, including brain scans, were introduced after the death of Johnny Owen. But no matter what health checks are introduced, the nature of the sport makes such tragedies occasionally inevitable. All that can be done is to make the sport as safe as possible.

Blaming himself for what happened, Gardiner quit the fight game for two years, only to make a return to prove a point to himself and family and take a fighter to a World title, not just for himself but for Johnny Owen.

He was to achieve that first with Steve Robinson, the WBO

featherweight champion, and then with Robbie Regan, who won the WBO bantamweight crown. Those victories were as much for Owen as himself and in the moment of their triumphs it was to the battling Owen his thoughts turned to.

"I never want Johnny to be forgotten," says Gardiner. "He was a great fighter and a great ambassador for the sport. A lot of kids looked up to Johnny Owen because he was a person who believed in himself and his sport."

He was also the most dedicated trainer Gardiner has ever met. He worked hard at his craft and his fitness. Boxing was his life and it was what he was happiest at and where he excelled.

The Owen family have never really recovered. Owen's mother had been dubious about her son taking part in the sport and it was his father who was keen. Gareth Jones, who knows the family, believes it was a factor in the break-up of the marriage shortly after.

For journalist Ken Jones, who has had a lifetime covering the sport around the world, it made him question whether he should continue at ringside. He found himself asking the question of whether it was all worth it.

"It is a serious question that makes me uncomfortable," he confessed. "There is a primitive and vicarious thrill with boxing, but I have no complaints with people who say it is not justified medically or morally. Yet I know I will be there the next time. And Johnny Owen would understand that."

The words of Merthyr-born Ken Jones, who attended the funeral, serve as an epitaph for Owen: "Early snow settled on the hills around Merthyr as though nature had sent a shroud for Johnny Owen; the valley had not forgotten how to dress for sadness: clouds grey and forlorn, the white flakes dissolving into grimy dampness on the streets of the town.

"Johnny Owen had come home the previous night, up through Rhymney and Tredegar, over Dowlais Top and then down to rest in a church at the bottom of the town. Of all the towns in the world, none seems better prepared for mourning."

On average, between eight and nine fighters a year die in the ring worldwide. Owen was not to be the last Celt to suffer such a fate. James Murray was buried on a bleak autumn afternoon. The service took place at Coltness Parish Church in Cambusnethan in the west of Scotland.

Murray's coffin was carried out of the church in silence. On top of the brass nameplate lay the dead boxer's Scottish bantamweight championship belt. When the prayers ended, the lone figure of a Scottish piper stepped forward and played *Scotland the Brave* and *Flower of Scotland*.

The boxer who had shared the ring with him on the tragic night, Drew Docherty, stood a short distance from the graveside staring as the coffin of Murray was carefully lowered. He was buried wearing his red robe.

Murray fought Docherty in the Grand Ballroom of the Holiday Inn in Glasgow's city centre for the British bantamweight title on Friday, 13 October 1995. Within a minute of the first round, Murray floored Docherty with a left hook. He looked ready to seize his big chance. His hope was to use the British title as a stepping stone for European and World honours. Docherty, though, quickly recovered and the contest settled down into a hard solid fight.

With only 45 seconds of the final round to go, Docherty threw two punches. The first caught Murray on top of his head. The second was aimed at his chest, but even before it landed James Murray was in trouble. He fell forward, as if in slow motion, on to the canvas. Sky television's ringside commentator screamed into his microphone: "Friday the 13th couldn't be more unlucky for James Murray."

Suddenly, Murray's left leg begins to shake violently. A cornerman stops it and holds it down. Then the boxer's torso starts to shake and convulse. He's clearly in severe agony. His mother, Margaret Murray, rushes out of her seat and starts screaming through the ropes: "Jimmy get up. Please Jimmy, get up."

Panic erupts inside the ring. A doctor attends to Murray. A riot among the drunken fans catches everyone unawares. The MC screams at the audience: "Pack it in! There's a boxer in trouble in the ring."

Finally a stretcher arrives as the riot takes hold. Glasses, bottles and chairs are thrown. Innocent bystanders are caught in the mayhem. The scenes are broadcast live by Sky TV as the ambulance heads across Glasgow towards Southern General Hospital in Govan. The riot was blamed on drunks who had been allowed to pay at the door and come into the arena. In the context of the death in the ring, the trouble pales into insignificance, but there is a determination there will be no repeat of such incidents in Glasgow.

Tommy Gilmore, the manager of Drew Docherty, believes the louts responsible were to be condemned and had brought shame on the city of Glasgow with the mayhem they caused being shown around the nation.

In the early hours of Saturday morning, surgeons attempted to save Murray's life by removing the blood clot from his brain. Despite their efforts, the operation was not successful. At 8.50am on Sunday, 15 October, Gareth Cruickshank, the hospital's consultant neurosurgeon, pronounced the boxer clinically brain dead and Murray's life support machine was switched off.

The family were paid the £5,000 fight fee and a £50,000 insurance fee under the British Boxing Board of Control's agreements for professional fighters who die through injuries sustained in boxing.

The boxer's father, Kenny Murray, now wishes the family had taken up the *Sun* newspaper's offer of tens of thousands of pounds for the story. "Jim would have wanted us to have done it," he says. "He knew how hard money was to come by."

Murray's heroes were the Panamanian Roberto Duran and Sugar Ray Leonard. Men who had risen from humble beginnings to be World champions. Murray dreamed of these men as he pushed himself to reach the heights in boxing.

At a press conference a few days after his son had died, Kenny Murray's message to other boxers was: "Keep boxing and stay off drugs. Remember Jim Murray did not die with a needle in his arm. He did not die up a back street."

In an ironic twist of fate, Barry McGuigan, the former World featherweight champion and boxing pundit for Sky, should have been commentating on the Murray fight but was instead the guest at Trinity College, Dublin, for a debate on whether boxing should be allowed. The articulate and popular former champion had won round the students and received a landslide backing in the debate. Back in his hotel, he received a phone call to say Murray was injured. He watched the fight and thought it was a tough one.

McGuigan attended the funeral and tried to offer some comfort to Mrs Murray. "I put my arm around her and said: 'It will be alright,' but how could it be when she had lost her son. It was a terrible time. I will never forget it. For something like that to happen in the ring was a tragedy."

He said all fighters had to be aware there was a chance

something could go wrong in the ring. It was always hoped that each death would be the last, but in a sport where the objective is to hit your opponent, there will always be risk, there will always be danger, and occasionally there will be serious injury and sometimes there will be fatalities.

For journalists like Jim Reynolds, boxing correspondent of the *Glasgow Herald*, who make their living from the sport, such tragedies affect him deeply. He recalls the terrible night and has nothing but sympathy for the families of both boxers. He does not believe a ban is the answer. The sort of unlicensed circuit where Ken Buchanan finished his career would be the outcome. He recalls the death of Murray as an awful time for boxing in Scotland, but the Murray family covered themselves with great dignity, especially in their support for Docherty. That was wonderful, he believes, and ensured Docherty continued his career.

Jim Murray was an ordinary working-class lad who, as a youngster, had been in some trouble, but had settled down when he discovered boxing. His ambition was to be a World champion and earn enough money to buy his parents a house and his sister a car. He worked as a landscape gardener, but was planning to box full time if he had won the fight with Docherty. Reynolds talked to Murray before the fight, when he was laughing and joking. He was confident of beating Docherty and a lot of people thought he would have the edge. His career had seemed about to take off and the presence of the television cameras would have raised his profile.

His manager, Alex Morrison, who also promotes in Glasgow, admits that when Murray first went down in the fight he was disappointed because, from the way he tired, he believed his boxer had not been training properly. Then he realised something was wrong. It was the next day before he was told Murray wasn't going to recover.

He remembers a dedicated boxer who dreamed of reaching the heights. Murray lived off his wages and saved everything he had earned from boxing. He had a good career ahead of him and was a talented fighter.

Tommy Gilmore, who manages Drew Docherty, says the fighter became introverted after the fight but the boxers with whom he trains and his family rallied round to support him. The support of the Murrays was another important factor in helping him recover. For Docherty there was the decision of whether to continue. He has boxed since he was 11 years old and it is his life. He has made friends through the sport and was in the 1988 Olympic team.

There is also the awareness that to quit means returning to a humdrum low-paid job and the end of the £1,000 purses he has become used to. He has a wife and young daughter to support.

The death of Murray was the worst tragedy he had to face in his life. He considered giving up the sport that had meant so much. In the end the support of the Murray family persuaded him to continue and he hopes that if he can win the World title, it will reflect some credit on James Murray. Show that he was a world-class fighter.

Three months after Murray's death, Docherty fought for the WBO World bantamweight title against the champion, Daniel Jimenez from Puerto Rico. Docherty battled bravely over 12 rounds, only to lose a points decision. The Murrays are genuinely sad he did not win.

At the end of the bout, standing beside the ring still sweating from the fight, Docherty was interviewed by a ring-side commentator. "I wasn't only fighting for myself tonight," he says, "I was fighting for ..." and then his voice breaks off. He starts to cry.

In the front room of the Murrays' home, a large picture of Jim dominates and his boxing trophies are on display. Kenny Murray defends the sport that took his son's life, but also gave him so much.

"It changed him and gave him more self-confidence," he said. "When he was a youngster he was a bit of a tearaway but he settled down and became dedicated to the sport. He enjoyed training and worked hard. Boxing was his life."

They have met the Docherty family and do not blame boxing for what happened. They wish Drew well in his career. Kenny Murray said: "Jimmy Murray did not have to fight for money. He had a job. It was more than the cash. He wanted to be good. He wanted to be special. He hoped to be successful and make people sit up and take notice."

Docherty still hopes for another shot at a World title. This time the bantamweight crown of the Welshman Robbie Regan. Twice the fight has been cancelled due to Regan being ill. In the meantime there is the chance of a European title challenge. The hardest game goes on.

Chapter Ten

Barry McGuigan and the Marketing of a Fighter

O N a cold wet night in a Dublin football stadium in May 1981, a young boxer from Clones, County Monaghan, was starting his professional career. Barry McGuigan and his manager, Barney Eastwood, were to bring big-time boxing back to Belfast.

McGuigan, though, would achieve more than that. His popularity spread way beyond the city where he did much of his early fighting. The Irish featherweight became a global boxing figure.

Two hundred million people worldwide saw him take the

World title from Eusebio Pedroza. He was one of the first boxers to herald in the new era of big box office boxing backed by satellite television.

It all seems a far cry from the night in Dublin when his first professional opponent was a journeyman pro called Selvin Bell with the far-from-wonderful record of 42 defeats in 58 fights. It was a one-way affair lasting only until an uppercut in the second round ended proceedings.

The television cameras were at the contest, but not to see the young McGuigan. On that evening, the career of an Irish champion was being brought to a brutal end. Charlie Nash had taken one fight too many.

Nash was defending his European title against Joey Gibilisco, an Australian-based Sicilian, and was taking a beating. The Irishman was knocked-out in the sixth round. By the time the ambulance taking him to hospital had arrived at its destination, the friends and family of McGuigan were celebrating his victory as though he had won a title.

As the boxer's career progressed, a cleverly orchestrated public relations campaign created the image of McGuigan as the 'Peacemaker' with the dove of peace on his shorts. He was portrayed as the man whose achievements united the divided communities of Northern Ireland.

Cynics may argue that the whole peace image was little more than a gimmick and that boxing has always easily crossed the sectarian divide. The Irish international amateur team is drawn from the 32 counties and in the professional game the crowds never showed any of the sectarian bitterness which marked so much of everyday life in Belfast.

In March 1983, a packed King's Hall in Belfast staged a contest between two Irishmen for the British bantamweight title. The fight split the city. The champion, Hugh Russell, drew his support from the Catholic New Lodge district of Belfast, with the Protestant challenger, Davy Larmour, enjoying the Loyalist backing of the Shankhill population. Despite the intense rivalry between them, to the credit of the boxers and supporters, no attempt was made to exploit their religious differences.

For McGuigan, the peacemaker image was powerfully emotive and effective and the British media, who for years had handled nothing but bad and bloody news from Northern Ireland, suddenly had a "'feel good' story on their hands and it made great copy for national newspapers.

Here was the young boxer who crossed the sectarian divide to unite the warring factions. The battler for unity. The flag of peace, carried into the ring and later to become part of the McGuigan trappings, was in fact adapted from the symbol of the Holiday Inn in London, where the McGuigan camp stayed prior to a fight at the Albert Hall.

Yet as McGuigan points out, even if only for the time he was fighting, and perhaps only on a dozen occasions, both sides of the sectarian divide were united in their support for him and were bonded to a common cause. In the troubled 1980s he was perhaps the only man who would be acclaimed in both the Loyalist Shankhill and Republican Falls Road areas of Belfast.

McGuigan is proud that he brought some harmony however briefly. "It was wonderful that happened. Those nights at the King's Hall were special occasions. It might have involved only a few thousand people, but for the evening at least differences were forgotten."

McGuigan was born south of the border and he was aware even from his amateur days that he would attract support from those north of the border who considered themselves British and those in the Republic who were Irish.

His amateur career had taken him to a gold medal at the Commonwealth games in Montreal in 1978. It was during this time that he was watched by Barney Eastwood, who thought he would be better suited to the longer distance contests in the paid ranks.

Shortly after he fought in the Olympics in Moscow in 1980, McGuigan turned professional. There had been offers from leading managers Mickey Duff and Terry Lawless, but it was to the bookmaker from Belfast he went. Eastwood persuaded him to become a British subject in order that he might win a British title. This would help in matchmaking and the title would also be an important stepping stone on the way to greater things.

Becoming British champion would enhance his marketability in Belfast, Eastwood's operational headquarters and home to the King's Hall. The arena is one of boxing's great venues and with Eastwood doing the hard sell to the media, the great Belfast fight nights began. By mid-1982 the McGuigan phenomenon was established and he had created his own unique aura.

The flag was largely to resolve what was a clear conundrum for McGuigan. At this time it was the fashion for boxers to arrive in the ring with their national flag. For McGuigan that would have been the flag of the Irish Republic. Its arrival in Belfast would clearly antagonise a good section of the audience.

"The flag of peace cut out all the political connotations," says McGuigan, "and it allowed us to remain apolitical. We felt that was very important, not as a gimmick but to be receptive to everybody's feelings. People who supported me would be British or Irish and they would all be from my homeland as it were."

Instead of a national anthem, McGuigan's father, Pat, who had represented Ireland in the Eurovision song contest, sang *Danny Boy* which became a feature of the McGuigan fights.

The boxer knows that cynics believe it was done as a marketing exercise, but it was not that trivial. It not only galvanised his support but, as he says: "It ensured people who never travelled together or went out together because of their religion, arrived and supported me together. That was a unique response."

It also ensured that when he went to the ring, he received a tumultuous reception that lifted McGuigan and had opponents unnerved. Particularly when the contest was in the cauldron that is the King's Hall.

Harry Mullan, editor of *Boxing News*, was at McGuigan's first professional fight and had seen him during his amateur career. "We were always aware that he was a unique talent from a young age and that view was enhanced when he won his gold medal at the Commonwealth games."

He recalls meeting McGuigan and his manager Eastwood on the afternoon before his second professional fight. It was for afternoon tea in an hotel and Mullan remembers that McGuigan was very shy and a far cry from the sophisticated and articulate television commentator of today.

The main thrust of the meeting revolved around a discussion between Mullan and Eastwood over what colour shorts the fighter should wear: green to show that he was Irish and proud of it; or a neutral blue that would be more diplomatic. Eastwood decided on blue.

A small matter but a clear indication that from the very early days, the shrewd mind of Eastwood was leaving nothing to chance when it came to the marketing of his boxer.

Mullan believes that McGuigan was probably the best packaged fighter these shores have produced. "There was a whole public relations edifice built up around McGuigan. It was a brilliant promotional exercise by Eastwood. The whole peacemaker image was a PR myth. McGuigan did nothing for any long-term unification in Northern Ireland."

His career was going well. There had been a surprise defeat that owed more to a bad decision by the referee than any lapse on McGuigan's part and Eastwood was happy with the way things were progressing. Then disaster struck in his 12th professional fight. The most distressing episode in McGuigan's fight career and the memory of which still haunts him was a tragic encounter with the Nigerian Alimi Mustafa, who boxed under the name Young Ali.

In June 1982, Young Ali was knocked-out in the sixth round before an exclusive audience at the World Sporting Club in London's Mayfair. He collapsed in his manager's arms on leaving the ring. For five months he lay in a coma. When he died it had a devastating effect on McGuigan. He thought long and hard about giving up boxing altogether but concluded: "Boxing is a risk business. It could have been me who was badly injured that night. Boxing is my whole life. It's the only livelihood I have, so I have to carry on and try to forget that tragic incident."

McGuigan still remembers the death and says it was hard to cope. "I am an emotional and sensitive person. For a long time I was disenchanted with the sport. I was confused and didn't know what to do."

After much deliberation he decided that he would fight on and that if he won the title, he would dedicate it to Young Ali.

And McGuigan recalls: "When I beat Pedroza and was World champion amid all the celebrations, he was the first thing I thought about."

Mullan believes the death of Young Ali was something McGuigan never got over and its affect was particularly damaging because it happened so early in the boxer's career. He remembers interviewing McGuigan for the boxer's autobiography and when everything else had been discussed, the question of Young Ali was raised.

"It was," says Mullan, "one of the most moving conversations I have had. McGuigan looked at his hands, crying, and said: 'I can't believe I killed a man with these.' It was a powerful and moving moment. I know what happened in the ring that night will scar him deeply as long as he lives."

McGuigan carried on boxing and continued his winning ways. He won the British title, beating Vernon Penprase to become the first Irishman to hold the championship since Billy 'Spider' Kelly in 1956. He won with a convincing knock-out in the second and quashed any doubts that the trauma of Young Ali would cause him to hold back on knock-out punches.

The European title was won with a victory over Valerio Nati which set him up for the World title chance. It had been a long time coming for the Irish fight fans. It was nearly 25 years since Johnny Caldwell had won a World title.

McGuigan captured the WBA featherweight title at Loftus Road, London, on 8 June 1985. The 'Clones Cyclone' dethroned one of the great champions of the modern era in Eusebio Pedroza, who was making his 20th defence of the title — the second-best record this century.

Pedroza had declined to come to Belfast, which given the support the Irishman would have generated in the King's

Hall seemed obvious enough. What he probably had not anticipated was that 26,000 people would cross the Irish Sea to cheer on their hero.

With a purse for McGuigan of £150,000, the fight was staged in London. As he walked out, McGuigan remembers feeling initially that the crowd was not as vociferous as usual, but that was because of the open-air venue compared to the King's Hall.

McGuigan's pre-fight preparations had not been without their setbacks. He had been suffering from a cold for a few days and had damaged a ligament in an elbow five days earlier. Nothing, though, was going to rob him of his big night.

By the time he reached the ring there were people trying to break down the barriers and the reception from the 27,000 crowd was deafening. McGuigan remembers the intensity of the fans was incredible.

The champion from Panama had a reputation for durability and certainly plenty of experience. The fight set off at a furious pace. Harry Carpenter, commentating for the BBC, said the pace couldn't continue, but it did. McGuigan had practised body punches in order to force the champion to drop his elbow and give a target.

In the seventh round the plan worked and the Irishman landed a blow to the chin that had Pedroza on the floor and in trouble. McGuigan tried to capitalise but the champion's ring craft enabled him to hold the challenger in a clinch and he survived. McGuigan, though, knew the fight was his if he could keep his head.

Pedroza was down in the ninth and was again in trouble in the 13th.

McGuigan knew he was ahead on points, but wanted to

finish it before then. As the fight wore on, he lost track of time.

He remembers: "I asked what round it was and my corner told me I had three minutes to become World champion. I won the fight on a unanimous decision and it seemed like the whole of London was celebrating."

When the final bell went he embraced Pedroza. McGuigan cannot remember what he said, but he knows what the former champion said to him: "You'll be a good champion."

The worldwide audience saw the man rated by some commentators as the best pound-for-pound boxer of his day establish his reputation not just in Britain, but in America as well.

It had cost Eastwood the best part of $1 million to lure the champion to London to defend his title. He recalls having seen Pedroza fight five times before agreeing to the match. On four of them he had returned to Belfast thinking it was far too much of a chance putting McGuigan in with him. On the last time he saw him, he thought Pedroza was on the slide and a good young fighter had a chance of beating him.

"Against McGuigan, the champion put up a good show and it was a good fight," says Eastwood. "He had troubles making the weight, which was all in our favour. I was pleased that everything had gone right."

With the victory, a wildly cheering crowd of some 40,000 lined the main streets of Belfast to welcome the conquering hero, while the entire population of Clones turned out for his home town arrival. In Dublin there was also a huge response. The police had expected around 25,000 for the lunchtime parade through the city centre to the Mansion

House, where McGuigan was welcomed by Lord Mayor Michael O'Halloran.

In fact more than 100,000 jammed the route of the open-topped bus, bringing traffic to a standstill. It was a comparable crowd to the one that a few years earlier had welcomed Pope John Paul II.

McGuigan repaid the fans for their loyalty and support by making the first two defences of his title in Ireland, even though he could have made more money fighting in the United States or even in England.

Belfast was first. McGuigan had a compulsory defence against Bernard Taylor, whose record was good enough to have included fighting Pedroza to a draw. The American started at a furious pace and was winning the opening rounds.

McGuigan started to get on top and in the seventh round landed a good body shot and then followed up with a right and left just before the round ended. Taylor did not come out for the next round.

Dublin was next, with the first World title fight in the city since Mike McTigue beat Battling Siki 63 years earlier. Danilo Cabrera of the Dominican Republic was the opponent. The 15 February date coincided with an Ireland rugby international and the city was buzzing.

An American television channel had taken over a bar opposite the fight venue and was providing free Guinness in return for the chance to capture the atmosphere of a real Irish watering hole and get the locals' views on McGuigan. Audiences in the United States could not get enough of the Irish World champion.

Cabrera became the first fighter to show any chinks in the Irishman's armour. McGuigan liked to come forward but was less effective if an opponent was strong enough to force him on to the retreat. In the eighth the champion suffered a cut eye.

McGuigan was strong enough to fight back and in coming forward Cabrera left too many openings. The champion won in the 14th but was badly marked around the eyes and had to have six stitches in one wound.

It was the chase for the fast buck that proved disastrous for Barry McGuigan. Eastwood agreed to a title defence in Las Vegas on 23 June 1986. The decision to fight in the desert, in the heat of the day under a blinding sun, was without question a major blunder, but America was where the major money was to be made. A completely drained McGuigan wilted under unbearable conditions to lose a unanimous points verdict to the challenger, Steve Cruz. The 100 degree heat had done more than cost the champion his title. He was rushed to hospital suffering from dehydration and spent the night in intensive care.

What surprises many is that McGuigan fought at that time of day when he did not need to. He was the top fight on the bill and his camp could have dictated the time they fought.

The defeat signalled the end for the partnership between Barney Eastwood and Barry McGuigan, a partnership which had seemed so idyllic to outsiders at least. The financial details surrounding the fight began to come under scrutiny. It prompted a great deal of controversy and a lengthy legal battle that saw the boxer stay out of the ring for more than a year while the managerial trouble was sorted out.

It became apparent that there had been a long souring of relations between the two. Both blame the other for the Las Vegas contest. The differences go back further. Eastwood said he blamed outside advisers who were looking to promote McGuigan and were giving him advice he would have been better not to have heeded. After the Cruz fight the former manager says 'everybody started playing the blame game'.

Both claim they would have preferred an alternative: a challenge for Wilfredo Gomez's WBA junior-lightweight title. A contest that would have preserved McGuigan's World crown whatever the outcome.

McGuigan says of the Cruz fight: "I was always unhappy about the fight and that is on record. I was ill-prepared for the fight when it took place and I wasn't myself when I was fighting. I didn't perform. I wasn't the normally sharp and robust self that people had seen before."

What makes it worse is that in his own mind he knows that if the circumstances leading up to the fight had been right, the result would have been different. At his best the Irishman would have had too much class for Cruz.

Eastwood, not surprisingly, sees things differently, claiming he never wanted McGuigan to fight outside Ireland. "I wasn't in boxing for the money. I had a lot of other businesses going and I was happy for him to continue boxing in Ireland and we would bring the challengers here. It was his decision to go there."

The manager and fighter, who had been together so long, were henceforth to confine their meetings to a courtroom. The legal battle has been well documented. Eastwood continues as a manager and has brought on a number of World champion successors to McGuigan.

He believes he is a good manager, and speaking about bringing on a World champion in general he says it needs a £100,000 outlay in expenses. Money that will be lost if the fighter doesn't make the grade.

In picking a boxer who might become a champion, he looks at a boxer's amateur career, his family and background and whether he has the quality and charisma that marks out a good World champion. Whatever their dispute there is no doubt that McGuigan had the right pedigree. And in an aside aimed at McGuigan, he says: "Once they are champion everybody tells them how much they should have earned. Once they get to the top they get a chip on their shoulder. Relationships don't work out."

He believes fighters who make it, do not give enough credit to the people who guided them to the top. "Without those people they would never have made it." In McGuigan's case, though, established managers like Lawless and Duff would have undoubtedly made sure he succeeded.

For the man from Clones, the Cruz fight and the legal aftermath effectively ended his career. The question of what he could have achieved but for that afternoon in the Nevada sun will forever remain unanswered.

For Mullan there is no doubt that, but for that experience, there were new heights to be scaled. In his view McGuigan had the potential to be the greatest fighter that came out of Ireland. Because of what happened in Las Vegas that potential was never really fulfilled.

McGuigan returned to the ring in 1987 with the legal situation resolved and the intention that if he could recapture his old form he could quickly regain a World ranking and challenge for a World title. Making the weight for the 9st division had always been something of a trial and the idea was to move up to the super-featherweight division.

Having eventually freed himself from his links with Eastwood and ironed out contractual obstacles, McGuigan now signed with Frank Warren and his first comeback fight was to be against the American Nicky Perez in London. Sparring and gym work went well and there were hopes that the legal difficulties would merely prove to be a pause in his career rather than a full-stop to it. It included a behind-closed-doors contest using the 8oz gloves worn in the fight ring rather than the heavier, more padded gloves usually used in training.

The private trial went well and then in the public arena, Perez was quickly accounted for. The referee stopped the fight in the fourth. It was followed with a fourth-round defeat against Tomas Da Cruz and for a moment the McGuigan show was back on the road.

The first big question-mark came in a bout against Julio Miranda, whose one defeat in 34 fights pointed to a much better pedigree than the previous two opponents. McGuigan was cut over both eyes and although he finally overpowered his opponent, it was not a vintage performance.

The end came in the fourth and last of the comeback fights. He received £250,000 to fight Jim McDonnell in Manchester. McGuigan was caught in the second round with a long left hook and the blood flowed. Referee Mickey Vann stepped in and that was the end of McGuigan's fight career. The badly cut eye needed seven stitches. That night he announced his retirement.

It had been a different fighter in the ring than the one who had thrilled millions on television and brought huge crowds at his fights to their feet. The built-in radar to see punches coming was gone, the edge taken off the reflexes. He had set high standards and was falling short of them.

Looking back on why the return failed, McGuigan explained: "Something was missing. I don't think the ambition was there. I worked very hard and put a lot of preparation into the fights, but the enthusiasm was gone. The Cruz fight took something out of me. There's a saying that fighters are always the last to know when to quit and I wanted to retire when I knew."

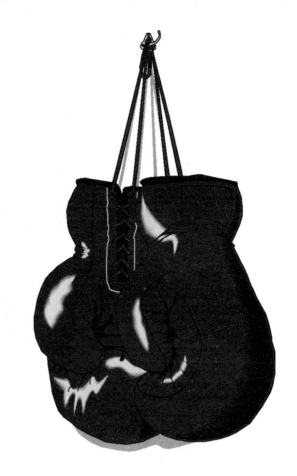

Chapter Eleven

Boxing As Box Office

AT present more than 130 boxers can claim to be World champions at some weight with various ruling bodies. When Tommy Farr stepped into the ring with Joe Louis in 1937, only eight men on earth could boast such a title.

Global television politics have generated the need for more and more big-time boxing. This requires more boxers and more champions. New weight limits have been introduced to produce a champion at a difference of every three pounds or so.

New governing bodies are formed out of alliances with rival television networks. Despite the initial derision, as a new body is introduced acceptance soon follows. When the IBF was formed in 1983 it was not taken seriously. The WBO was given much the same reception as the IBF. Now, thanks to Sky television, it is the biggest supplier of Celtic World champions.

Boxing still has its roots in the countless local clubs and gyms of working-class neighbourhoods. But now a sophisticated commercial structure channels local talent into national entertainment markets. Boxing has become big business. What commercial sophistication has given in breadth of audience appeal it has taken away in depth. Boxers are now celebrities, individuals who make careers out of offering a spectacle to paying audiences rather than being the folk heroes of local communities.

Boxing has become an exciting entertainment, sold on international leisure markets, similar to circuses, theme parks, the movies. Boxing has lost its old expressive force and, for all the money it generates, much of its popularity. Sanitised television performances sell. Local events promoted in clubs and halls are failing. The array of World titles have made the British championship, with its Lonsdale Belt, a devalued stepping stone on the way to greater things.

The days in the 1930s when there would be boxing shows in cities like Glasgow and Belfast most nights of the week are long gone. Many of the new breed of fight fans have never been to a live boxing event. Rather than support local talent, they prefer to see the packaged offerings on television. There are fewer boxers taking part. Those with a title that can guarantee one of the big-time shows can make a handsome living. For the rest, good pay days are hard to come by.

Although they still spring from tough neighbourhood subculture, boxers, especially the most successful ones, are decreasingly representative of their roots. Successful boxers have been turned into celebrities, new models of success in a culture dedicated to fame, leisure and consumption.

The biggest market continues to be the United States, and the Celts are still in big demand. Athletic heroes added a new dimension to America's success ethic. Champion boxers fulfilled the dream of personal achievement and unlimited individual opportunity. In the States the money generated is colossal. The heavyweight division still attracts the big bucks, but in the lighter weights boxers who capture the public eye can still profit handsomely.

Oscar De La Hoya is unbeaten in 24 fights, has already won World titles at four weights and is being touted as the world's best pound-for-pound fighter. An undoubtedly talented boxer, he is also handsome. — and hence good box office. It means at 24 he has already earned $50 million.

In Britain, the biggest draw is Prince Naseem Hamed, the IBF and WBO featherweight champion. He is famous for his power-punching and his gloriously choreographed entrance to the ring. In these modern times you need a gimmick.

The late Eddie Thomas, a man imbued with the spirit of the fight game, had little doubt about why the showbusiness element has arrived. It points to a lack of talent at the work-face itself. "The class has gone out of boxing," in his opinion.

Given he was a British, European and Empire welter-weight champion and managed both Howard Winstone and Ken Buchanan to World crowns, he may have known what he was talking about.

But time has a habit of playing funny tricks.

The new array of weight divisions would have been ideal for Thomas, as they are for many others. Now the fate of nature cannot play such a big part. Thomas struggled to make the 10st 7lbs limit of the welterweight and had to endure the misery of trying to sweat off the pounds. Yet attempting to make middleweight, at 13bs heavier would have put him against much bigger men and at a huge disadvantage. Fighting 50 years on, he could have been accommodated at his natural weight of 11st in the light-middleweight division.

Talk of razzmatazz as something new to disguise lack of talent is also way off the mark. Others were there before and a long time ago. The best, or worst, who springs to mind is Jack Doyle, the Irish heavyweight of the 1930s who was more than happy to cash in on good looks and a fine singing voice to hype his boxing career. It was just as well. In the boxing talent stakes he was woefully limited.

In the last century, the men who reached the top were in no mood to relinquish their title. Most were happy to shield the crown from genuine contenders and fight no-hopers. Or take to the stage in vaudeville performances and specially written melodramas.

Boxing has always been a hard game and those who partake of it to rise from the poverty of their backgrounds generally see nothing wrong in cashing in while they can, in what is inevitably a short and demanding career. Certainly Barry McGuigan, who some say ushered in the new age of big-money televised boxing, can lament, tongue-in-cheek, that he was born ten years too early. If he had been born in 1971 rather than 1961, he would now be squaring up to Prince Naseem Hamed and enjoying multi-million pound pay days.

"Things have changed dramatically and for the good," he argues. "Sky's arrival has hugely magnified boxing. The money has come along and from my point of view as an ex-boxer and the president of the Professional Boxers' Association, that has been a benefit."

The proliferation of titles has also meant more opportunities for fighters to get a decent pay day. The days when British champions like Ken Buchanan had to fight for such derisory pay days in Britain that they threatened to hand the title back and return to a nine-to-five job does not point to a halcyon age long gone. The satellite television rivalry has also ended the incestuous relationship which developed between a cabal of major promoters and managers and the BBC that ensured only fighters from their stables in matches under their control got the much-needed television exposure that guaranteed a high profile and decent pay days. Rose-tinted spectacles have their place and it is gathering dust in the bottom draw somewhere.

As Steve Collins, the current WBO super middleweight champion, argues, it is not the officiating body for the title that matters, but the boxer.

Jingoistic fans who want to believe British is best can cheer a champion despite him never venturing anywhere near a rival title holder of quality or a genuine contender. Particularly one residing in the United States. Those who like the gimmicks and the showbiz element can be happily entertained. The music and the light show is usually very impressive. And the real fight fans, as Collins argues, will know which boxer is the true champion, whichever letters accompany his title.

And Collins should know. He is very much a fighter of the old school. The Celtic Warrior image and the shamrock cut into his hair may play the public relations game, but they are a far cry from the showman he superseded. The new hyped star is Hamed and he may prove to have the talent to back the taunts he is so quick to level at opponents. But he inherited the mantle as the public's popular champion, or most irritating fighter, depending on individual preference, from Chris Eubank, of monocle and Harley Davison fame. Eubank's pay days ended when he met Collins, a boxer short on gimmicks, but rather longer on ability.

Steve Collins followed in the footsteps of the great Irish boxing pioneers and crossed the Atlantic to build a successful career. He joined the Petronelli brothers in Boston and went on to win the Irish middleweight championship by beating Sam Storey

He learnt his trade sparring with some of the best and built up a popular following in his own right, particularly among the Irish communities of Boston and New York where he did most of his fighting.

Collins had fought and lost two World title challenges, but gained some kudos for both. He lost on points for the WBA middleweight World crown to the more than useful Mike McCallum in 1990. He also lost a split points decision for the vacant WBA title to Reggie Johnson in 1992. The boxer born in Dublin finally realised his title ambitions when he stopped Chris Pyatt inside five rounds to win the WBO title in 1994. The victory was played down because it was considered Pyatt was past his best.

The most glamorous weight division at the time was super middleweight. The presence of Chris Eubank and Nigel Benn as World champions for different bodies ensured a number of high-profile, big box office bouts. Huge television audiences could be assured.

The first to gatecrash the Eubank party was Irishman Ray Close from Belfast. Under the guidance of Barney Eastwood, he took the champion to a hard-fought draw and ensured himself a re-match.

Close lost the second fight, but the margin of defeat was narrow enough to ensure that he had a third lucrative bout with Eubank on St Patrick's Day, 1995. A few weeks before the fight, however, an abnormality on a brain scan ended Close's career. With tickets to sell for the title fight in Dublin, the promoters were in need of an Irishman who could give the unbeaten Eubank a good fight. Collins, the self-styled Celtic Warrior, answered the call.

After years of being a top-level performer mainly in the USA, Collins was thrust into the UK limelight. He may have been relatively unknown in this country, but the calibre of opponents he had faced should have sounded warning bells in the Eubank camp, particularly as their own man had been turning in increasingly mediocre performances.

Collins was 30 and was moving up eight pounds from his natural fighting weight. A win would bring not only status but a millionaire bank balance. He took his opportunity with both gloves and was elevated from replacement to the big-money league overnight. To train for the fight, Collins returned to the United States and set up camp in Las Vegas for a six-week training programme. There were to be no flutters on the gaming table. He concentrated on the task in hand.

When he returned to Ireland for the fight in March 1995, the country was already ready to cheer a home-grown fighter. Around 3,000 fans turned up for the weigh-in alone to see him taunt Eubank. In a touch of kidology, Collins claimed he was using hypnosis to make himself invincible. An already troubled Eubank seized on the claim, declaring it unfair and potentially dangerous. He even considered calling the fight off.

At the fight itself, with an audience approaching 14 million, the Eubank entrance was again its usual spectacular affair. this time arriving on a Harley Davison which was lowered from the air with the bike being highly revved and his signature tune of *Simply the Best* at high volume.

For the champion, though, the fight itself was not as impressive because Collins, who had sat on his corner stool with the hood of his robe over his face for the Eubank arrival, now set about the job in hand with a relish. Eubank found the challenger keeping him under constant pressure, a hustling scrapper against a champion determined to box at his own pace. When they came, the better punches were from the champion but the quantity came from Collins and they were pushing him ahead on the scorecard.

A right to the body put Eubank down and had the crowd roaring — certainly those prepared to support their local Irish fighter. But as one local journalist was disgusted to discover, many preferred the high-profile Eubank. It would never have happened in the old days.

After his spell on the canvas, the champion fought back. In the tenth it was the Irishman's turn to go down, this time from a right hook. The champion had fought back well to try and keep his title but it was not enough. Collins won a split decision and in a re-match four months later was a more convincing points winner.

The man who nobody noticed when he defeated Pyatt was now a household name. He had followed his forefathers to America to seek fame and fortune, but found it on his own doorstep. Satellite television now made anything possible.

If the tale of the Celtic Warrior has the makings of a Hollywood screenplay, the Steve Robinson story would be considered too far-fetched to have any credibility, although there are echoes of Sylvester Stallone's Rocky in the late replacement finding glory.

The story begins in a gym at Fleur-de-Lys in the Rhymney Valley, South Wales, run by the boxing trainer and manager Dai Gardiner, whose own boxing career had been cut short by eye trouble, but who had a talent for training and managing young fighters.

He produced a stable of promising boxers from his gym, but the star pupil was the bantamweight from the Gellideg Estate in Merthyr Tydfil, Johnny Owen. Owen lost his life in challenging Lupe Pintor for the title in Los Angeles and a heartbroken Gardiner turned his back on the sport for several years. It was the appearance of another prodigiously talented young boxer that persuaded him to try once more to produce a World champion.

Robbie Regan was born in Caerphilly and turned professional just before his 21st birthday. His career was going to schedule, with the British title won in only his eighth contest and then he took the European title. The path to a World crown seemed laid out when suddenly Gardiner's plans were sidelined by an unexpected telephone call in April 1993 that was to thrust another of his boxers, Steve Robinson, into the limelight.

Sky television had paid a fortune to Ruben Palacio of Colombia to go to Newcastle to defend his WBO featherweight title against the local favourite John Davison. The champion was tragically ruled out of the fight. His career ended when he failed the pre-fight AIDS test. The promoters and broadcasters were now left stranded a few days before the contest. The desperate attempt to find a fighter fit enough to take the bout at such short notice ended in Ely, Cardiff. Robinson, 24, was best known for being Regan's sparring partner. He did not feature in any of the World rankings. Indeed, he was rated no higher than the seventh-best featherweight in Britain.

Being brutally honest, Robinson was a once-a-month boxer who fought for small purses around the country and was fit enough to take any fight at any time. He had no place being anywhere near the ring for a World title contest. His record showed he had lost almost as many contests as he had won.

Gardiner remembers being in London at the time, negotiating a fight for Regan. He could see there was a panic while the promoter was looking for a replacement. They phoned everybody else and finally agreed on Robinson.

Robinson thought it was a hoax when he first got the call asking if he was available for the fight with Davison. He had recently given up his £52-a-week job as a storeman. He knew fighters with a record that shows nine defeats in 23 fights don't get such opportunities. His previous fight had been a disappointing points defeat in Paris against an unknown and unrated opponent. Unfortunately for Gardiner there were two immediate problems. Robinson was carrying a slight injury at the time.

And the pie and chips he was eating when the manager called did not sound the ideal culinary preparation for a title fight at short notice. The advice was to the point. The boxer had to check his weight to make sure he could make the 9st limit and then go for a six-mile run to see how the injury stood up. "I told him to ring me back within an hour because there was not much time," says Gardiner.

Robinson was reminded by Gardiner that such opportunities rarely came along and if he had come through the run all right he should take the title chance. There had been hopes of getting a European title fight. This was beyond belief. Robinson himself says at first he hesitated, not knowing whether he would be fit enough, but then decided he had to have a crack at the World title. "Even if I had lost I could say it was to a World champion. That would always be on my record."

The best the promoters were hoping for was a reasonable

performance. An early knock-out would be disastrous for the promoter and for the credibility of the WBO.

Within 48 hours of receiving the phone call, Robinson was face-to-face with Davison on live television and the boxing story of the decade unfolded before a disbelieving Geordie crowd expecting to proclaim their home-town man as champion.

It seemed Robinson had not had time to read the script. He started confidently and took the first four rounds before starting to tire, but then staged a rally towards the end.

Davison kept trying to land the big punch that would finish it but without success. As he became more desperate, the more the Welshman took control.

There was little doubt about the result handed down by the judges. Against all the odds, with very little preparation and cheered on by a minibus full of supporters, Steve Robinson became World champion. He was hoisted on to the shoulders of his cornermen including trainer Gardiner. An unforgettable moment in the fighter's life.

For the new champion, any thoughts of a celebration in the North-East were dispensed with. There was space in the minibus that had brought his supporters and that was good enough for Robinson as he headed back to South Wales through the night.

Gardiner was full of praise for his fighter who had shown 'great courage, strength and determination'. Yet as he celebrated with Robinson that night, his jubilation was tinged with sadness. Inevitably, his thoughts flashed back to his first World title challenger more than 12 years before. "I came back into the sport to prove that I was good enough to train a World champion," says Gardiner.

Robinson went on to defend his title seven times for

increasingly large purses. The man who had gone straight into the paid ranks in 1989 and gambled on turning full-time professional had made the big time. His last hurrah was to be more than two years later against the new king of satellite television, the 21-year-old Prince Naseem Hamed in a million pound extravaganza in Cardiff in 1995. The venue was Cardiff Rugby Club and a smattering of rain greeted the fighters for the outdoor event.

Robinson had been forced to cut short his honeymoon to begin his training after promoter Frank Warren refused to delay the date, which had given an edge to the contest and the 16,000 supporters were there to give the Cardiff man their vocal support.

The Prince outclassed the champion, who struggled to land his punches against the darting figure in front of him. In the fifth, a four-punch combination put him down. He survived, but the punches rained down on him for the next two rounds before a left hook ended it in the eighth.

The rise of Robinson to the big-money purses has not been without its problems. A contractual dispute with promoter Frank Warren saw him lose £100,000. But the man who was stacking shelves at a department store before his night of glory is now comfortably off.

The plethora of titles and weights has not tinged the delight at winning the World championship for Robinson and he believes that for the boxers the diversification has helped increase opportunities. "For me it took nothing away from winning the title and the more opportunities there are, the more it gives boxers a chance to make a decent living."

Despite the battering he took, Robinson wants a rematch with the hard-hitting Prince from Sheffield. He accepts he was a clear second-best on the night but, like all fighters, thinks next time may be different. Whether Hamed will accommodate him is open to debate.

Meanwhile, Wales was not to be without a World champion for long. Gardiner had always thought Robbie Regan would be a World champion. He had talent from an early age. He could box four or five different ways and was very clever, very strong and powerful. His chance had seemed to slip away when he lost to the Mexican Alberto Jiminez for the WBO World flyweight title.

His day, though, was still to come. Regan stepped out of the shadow of Robinson to take the bantamweight crown from Daniel Jimenez in front of a partisan crowd in Cardiff in April 1996. The tears flowed as the championship belt was strapped to him.

Jiminez was a worthy champion and it proved a hard fight for the Welshman. The speed and jab of the champion caused problems for Regan early on, but the challenger's heavier punching soon began to tell.

Towards the close of the eighth round, a heavy left hand caught the champion on the jaw. Jiminez beat the count but only just, rising on nine. The bell saved him before Regan could call a halt to the night's work. Willed on by the crowd, Regan charged forward for four more rounds. He did not land the knock-out blow, but all three judges had the home fighter ahead. It was the turn of another of Gardiner's boxers to have his life transformed as he entered the big time of world boxing.

The Welshman should have fought Drew Docherty, who was involved in the bout in which James Murray was killed, but twice Regan was forced to pull out through illness. "I feel sorry for both the fighters. We are contracted to make the fight and hopefully we will go ahead," says Gardiner.

As it had been since the days of Wilde, Driscoll and Welsh, it was at the lightest weight divisions that the Celts continued to thrive. The new titles opened up a wealth of opportunities which fighters from Wales, Scotland and Ireland were more than happy to take advantage of.

For much of the early part of Dave McAuley's career, the spotlight was on his more illustrious stablemate Barry McGuigan. Although he may have been overshadowed by the Clones Cyclone, McAuley owes much of his subsequent success to the former featherweight champion. McGuigan's manager Barney Eastwood also handled McAuley and had formed very close business links with powerful and influential figures in Panamanian boxing. Their association proved mutually rewarding during the years of McGuigan's triumphs.

It was also these contacts which enabled Eastwood in 1987 to arrange for McAuley, then a virtual unknown in world terms, to challenge the Panamanian Fidel Bassa for the WBA title in the King's Hall, Belfast. No one gave the inexperienced Irishman even an outside chance of victory, and the pessimism looked well founded when McAuley was floored in the opening round. Yet he fought back so effectively that he came agonisingly close to the championship and the contest was named Fight of the Year in 1987.

McAuley put Bassa on the floor five times in all but had spent himself in an effort to knock-out the champion. It was a superlative effort by the Irishman in a fight that was shown live on BBC TV. The man who had conducted his career hitherto in near anonymity found himself a star. His days of playing the supporting role on Barry McGuigan's fight nights were over.

A rematch with Bassa was a big attraction, but proved a

disappointment. The champion did just enough to stay out of trouble and won a points decision.

McGuigan's dispute with Eastwood had induced McAuley to consider his own position carefully and when he totalled his ring earnings from a four-year career and found them considerably short of what he regarded as adequate, he aired his grievances publicly in a series of sensational newspaper articles.

In print he vowed never to fight again if he had to do so under Eastwood's management. But privately talks were under way and peace was eventually restored. The price of the truce was a World title opportunity against the English-man Duke McKenzie, which Eastwood was able to deliver.

With the fighting outside the ring duly completed, it was now time to get back to the business in hand for McAuley. He took the IBF World title in June 1989 and reigned supreme until he was robbed of his crown by the Colombian, Rodolfo Blanco.

As McAuley lost one version of the flyweight title, Pat Clinton, from Croy, continued the great Scottish tradition in this weight division. Following a path blazed by fellow countrymen Benny Lynch, Jackie Paterson and Walter McGowan, Clinton took the WBO version of the flyweight title by beating Isidrio Perez in Glasgow.

The introduction of an even lighter weight division, the light flyweight, allowed another Scot, Paul Weir, to become his country's seventh World champion.

Irish boxers were also quick to seize upon the oppor-tunities offered by the new weight divisions and governing bodies. Eamon Loughran won a version of the World welter-weight title and Wayne McCullough headed for the bright lights of Las Vegas to become bantamweight champion.

McCullough was one of the stars of the Irish Olympic team that had a successful time in Barcelona in 1992. He was spotted by an American sports cable network who guided him to the World crown under the expert eye of the legendary trainer Eddie Futch.

The Olympic Games of 1996 may yet provide a similar platform for a young boxer to prove that the sport is the ultimate meritocracy: a violent world in which anyone can become someone.

Frank Barrett grew up without access to water, toilets and electricity. He did his best at primary school, but survived only a couple of years at Sister Bridget's secondary school for slow learners. "I'm not the best reader you could get," he says, "but I'm handy enough. I have a book in the caravan, I read one or two pages every night."

The Barrett boys raced ponies and collected scrap for their father. Then Frank discovered boxing. The local priest, Father Ned Crosby, was taking two traveller boys to a tournament in Ennis. The youngster pleaded to be allowed to go and was allowed. That evening Barrett met Chick Gillian, the local boxing coach. The two have been together ever since. With the help of the priest, Gillian set up the Olympic Boxing Club and although it was open to all, it was mostly travellers who turned up.

Barrett learned quickly, winning Irish titles at boys and youth levels. Success inspired him to train fiercely. Warming to his dedication, his own people got a disused 40ft-container and put it in a corner beside the caravan. Gillan fixed up a makeshift punchbag, someone else put up a colour photograph of Mother Teresa. The windowless container became his gym. He sparred there, skipped and shadow boxed and dreamed about the Olympic Games. He carried there the hopes of the traveller community and also an awareness that he had raised the standing of a group regarded as second class by many in Ireland.

Boxing proved for Barrett the way out. The only way out of a lifestyle where even today the life expectancy is shockingly low. Just five per cent of Irish travellers reach their 50th birthday.

Boxing allows men of poor backgrounds, armed only with a pair of gloves and raw courage to become heroes. For the few who reach the pinnacle, the rewards are many, yet most boxers leave the sport as poor and obscure as when they began.

In the Celtic nations there will still be many prepared to try. The booths may have gone and there are no longer boxing shows regularly held, but the ambition is still there. In Dai Gardiner's gym, boxers still work out and remember the example of Robinson and Regan who used the same punch bags. They hope their chance will come.

Index

INDEX